THE
MISTAKES
THAT
MAKE US

For information about this title or to place a bulk order for your organization, contact the publisher:

Constancy, Inc.
MarkGraban.com
Mark@MarkGraban.com
Book website: mistakesbook.com

ISBNs:
978-1-7335194-4-1 (hardcover)
978-1-7335194-5-8 (softcover)
978-1-7335194-6-5 (eBook)
978-1-7335194-7-2 (audiobook)

Printed in the United States of America

Developmental Editor: Tom Ehrenfeld
Cover Design: Don Coon
Book Coach: Cathy Fyock
Additional Editing and Interior Book Design: 1106 Design

Praise for

THE MISTAKES THAT MAKE US

*A full list of endorsements can be found at
mistakesbook.com.*

"Making mistakes is not a choice. Learning from them is. Whether we admit it or not, mistakes are the raw material of potential learning and the means by which we progress and move forward. Mark Graban's *The Mistakes That Make Us* is a brilliant treatment of this topic that helps us frame mistakes properly, detach them from fear, and see them as expectations, not exceptions. This book's ultimate contribution is helping us realize that creating a culture of productive mistake-making accelerates learning, confidence, and success."

—TIMOTHY R. CLARK, PhD, author of *The 4 Stages of Psychological Safety*, CEO of LeaderFactor

"At last! A book about errors, flubs, and screwups that pushes beyond platitudes and actually shows how to enlist our mistakes as engines of learning, growth, and progress. Dive into *The Mistakes That Make Us* and discover the secrets to nurturing a psychologically safe environment that encourages the small experiments that lead to big breakthroughs."

—DANIEL H. PINK, #1 *New York Times* bestselling author of *DRIVE, WHEN*, and *THE POWER OF REGRET*

"Mark's exhibition of errors not only acknowledges a core human experience that is frequently concealed but also fosters a feeling of togetherness among his audience, inspiring us to persevere in their pursuit of education and personal development."

—JIM McCANN, founder & chairman, 1-800-FLOWERS.COM, INC.

"In business, as in life, everyone makes mistakes. How we view and move on from mistakes can transform them from problems into opportunities for learning and growth. Mark's book delves into the ways we can use errors to help build and foster a culture of understanding and continuous improvement that embraces humanity as an integral part of work."

—ERIC RIES, author of *The Lean Startup* and *The Startup Way*

"Another useful book from Mark Graban! Creating the conditions to surface and learn from mistakes not only drives continuous improvement and innovation, but also good jobs. *The Mistakes That Make Us* shows us how to get there. I found his lessons useful for business and life."

—ZEYNEP TON, Professor of the Practice at MIT Sloan, President of Good Jobs Institute, and author of *The Case for Good Jobs: How Great Companies Bring Dignity, Pay & Meaning to Everyone's Work*

"At Menlo Innovations, one of our favorite phrases is 'Make Mistakes Faster!' It's not that we like making mistakes, we just prefer making small mistakes quickly rather than BIG mistakes slowly. The difference comes from creating a culture where we are safe to share our mistakes. Mark Graban teaches all of us how to do this and shares story after real story of the benefits. It would be a BIG mistake to ignore this wisdom!"

—RICHARD SHERIDAN, CEO & Chief Storyteller, Menlo Innovations, Author, *Joy, Inc.—How We Built a Workplace People Love* and *Chief Joy Officer—How Great Leaders Elevate Human Energy and Eliminate Fear*

"I can't recommend Mark Graban's book enough. Mark's candid storytelling and practical advice make this a must-read for anyone looking to navigate the ups and downs of their own journey. Whether you're just starting out in your career or a seasoned veteran, the book will inspire you to see failure not as something to be feared but as an essential part of the path to success. This is a book I'll be recommending to colleagues and friends for years to come."

—**BILLY RAY TAYLOR**, CEO of LinkedXL and author of *The Winning Link*

"Finally, a book that goes beyond noting the importance of growth and improvement and shows how embracing mistakes can lead us there. Ths book provides practical insights and real-world examples on how to foster a psychologically safe environment that encourages experimentation and innovation. The path to continuous improvement is there; learn how to embrace the bumpy road."

—**ETHAN BURRIS**, **PhD**, Niessa Professor of Management and Senior Associate Dean for Academic Affairs, McCombs School of Business at the University of Texas at Austin

"The path to success is paved with mistakes. And—as the Japanese proverb 'Fall down seven times, get up eight' represents—what matters is how we get up from the setbacks that knock us off course. We can all relate to—and learn from—the stories and insights in Mark's book, your guide for how to turn your mistakes into a pathway to success."

—**KATIE ANDERSON**, leadership consultant and author of *Learning to Lead, Leading to Learn*

"Dr. Deming told us to drive out fear. Toyota's model is respect for people and continuous improvement. They go hand in hand. Hiding mistakes is the death of continuous improvement. Mark uses stories to delve deeply into the disease and gives us powerful suggestions for creating an environment that breeds trust and high performance."

—**JEFFREY LIKER**, author of *The Toyota Way*

To the mistake-makers and those who help them.

ACKNOWLEDGMENTS

Thanks to my book coach, Cathy Fyock, for her encouragement and counsel. Thanks to my developmental editor, Tom Ehrenfeld—this book is significantly better because of his involvement (and I also thank him for reminding me to actively enjoy the writing process).

Thanks to Don Coon, a nearly lifelong friend and professional artist who volunteered to create the artwork for the *My Favorite Mistake* podcast and now this book. This cover isn't a "10" out of "10"—it goes to "11." I also thank Don for the gift of the word "cultivating" for the title, which inspired some of the metaphors and thinking around culture.

Thanks to all of my *My Favorite Mistake* podcast guests. I couldn't possibly have included everybody's stories and reflections in the book without it weighing more than a bowling ball. Every experience with a guest taught me something and helped me reflect on learning from mistakes. I appreciate your kindness and vulnerability. That helps so many people, not just me.

Thanks to sharp-eyed readers, including Kyle Kumpf, Mike Ulmer, Karyn Ross, John Saunders, Molly Rank, Jeff Liker, Jamie Flinchbaugh, P.L. Gowdre, and Alan Wikler, Psy.D. Some of them suffered through rough drafts, and everybody's input helped me iterate toward this final product. Thanks especially to Karyn for helping me understand (and articulate) the difference between being nice and being kind—and for demonstrating kindness.

Thanks to Kevin Goldsmith, Dan Garrison, Dr. David Mayer, Katie Anderson, Dr. Greg Jacobson, and David Meier for patiently helping me flesh out details of their stories and lessons learned beyond what we discussed in the podcast episodes.

Thanks to the entire team at KaiNexus for your willingness to share mistakes at work—and for allowing me to include them here. And thanks for cultivating a culture that ensures we'll keep speaking up about mistakes and, more importantly, learning from them.

Thanks to my parents, Bob and Marlene, for their lifelong support and encouragement of my curiosity, learning, and trying new things. Thanks to my in-laws, Charlie and Debbie, for long ago welcoming me into their family and for not concluding that it was a mistake.

Thanks, finally, and, most especially, to my amazing wife, Amy. Thanks for your love, support, and coaching as I take on projects like these. Thanks for the leadership you demonstrate to companies and the world. Make no mistake: I couldn't do this without you. Thanks for your sense of humor about the story you allowed me to bring from our kitchen to this book, and for not referring to me as your "favorite mistake." Love always . . .

ABOUT THE AUTHOR

Mark Graban has helped organizations improve for more than twenty-five years, in settings including manufacturing, healthcare, and software companies. He previously wrote or co-authored *Lean Hospitals, Healthcare Kaizen, Practicing Lean,* and, most recently, *Measures of Success: React Less, Lead Better, Improve More.* Working independently as a professional speaker and consultant, Mark is also a senior advisor to the technology company KaiNexus. He hosts multiple podcasts, including *Lean Blog Interviews* (started in 2006) and *My Favorite Mistake* (2020). Mark earned a BS in Industrial Engineering from Northwestern University and both an MS in Mechanical Engineering and an MBA from the MIT Sloan Leaders for Global Operations program. He and his wife, Amy, live wherever her career takes her.

Learn more and contact Mark through his website: MarkGraban.com, or email: Mark@MarkGraban.com

Also by Mark Graban

Lean Hospitals: Improving Quality, Patient Safety, and Employee Engagement (3rd Ed.)

Healthcare Kaizen: Engaging Front-Line Staff in Sustainable Continuous Improvements

The Executive Guide to Healthcare Kaizen: Leadership for a Continuously Learning and Improving Organization

Practicing Lean: Learning How to Learn How to Get Better . . . Better

Measures of Success: React Less, Lead Better, Improve More

Podcasts by Mark Graban

My Favorite Mistake

Lean Blog Interviews

Lean Whiskey

Lean Blog Audio

KaiNexus Continuous Improvement Podcast

Habitual Excellence, Presented by Value Capture

TABLE OF CONTENTS

INTRODUCTION

"What's your favorite mistake?"

When I asked 200 successful people that question, I learned that my podcast guests possess an admirable combination of confidence and humility. They have shared stories, reflections, and lessons, including:

- The member of Congress who lost his first primary before learning from his mistake and winning in his second try

- The CEO whose savvy acquisition literally made a name for his company but saddled it with a surprising debt load that might have been a blessing in disguise

- The retired Japanese Toyota executive who wasn't fired for a mistake that messed up the paint on 100 cars, and the American leader who had the same experience decades later in Kentucky

- The aide whose loose lips led to a spicy quote in *USA Today* but who, thankfully, worked for a U.S. Representative who focused on learning over punishment

- The distiller who over-aged 100 barrels of expensive whiskey but worked for a founder who realized mistakes happen when you're innovating

- The shark whose mistake almost put his company underwater for good . . .

Wait, a shark? That's not a typo. I'll explain it soon.

Why would people admit mistakes like these in a public forum? They understand how reacting kindly to mistakes can lead to growth and progress. They celebrate the progress and growth that results from mistakes when we react to them in constructive ways. My podcast and book are neither a pity party nor a shaming session. They are places to remember that we all make mistakes and to celebrate the learning and vulnerability that set a powerful example for others.

When people start a story with "I'm going to be vulnerable here," we often brace ourselves to hear something personal, if not embarrassing. Admitting a workplace mistake feels vulnerable because it exposes us to the risk of professional harm or loss—which could include being marginalized, demoted, or fired.

Guests on *My Favorite Mistake* admit and own their mistakes instead of blaming others for any misfortune. And they felt safe enough to do so. Sadly, many people feel pressured to protect themselves by keeping quiet about mistakes.

Speaking up isn't a matter of character or courage—it's driven by culture. People feel safe to share when their leaders and colleagues treat them with respect. Instead of asking people to be brave, leaders must create conditions where people can feel safe.

The most powerful question one can ask after a mistake is, "What did we learn?" People who know that their workplace reacts constructively to mistakes can reflect, learn, and improve—preventing mistakes from being repeated, learning how to prevent mistakes that haven't happened yet, and proactively improving every aspect of our work to drive better results.

POSITIVELY LEARNING FROM MISTAKES

Many say we learn the most from our mistakes and failures, including a certain beloved green character from a famous series of sci-fi galactic-adventure films, who said, "The greatest teacher, failure is." A fellow author warned me against possibly running afoul of a litigious entertainment company by mentioning the series' name. It does rhyme with, um, *Car Chores*.

Discussing mistakes might seem negative, but doing so helps us grow, leading to greater success. I'm positive about that. Mistakes can be turned into something positive—if we react to them the right way (being kind) and make the right adjustments (being constructive).

OFTEN, IT'S THE MISTAKES THAT MAKE US WHO WE ARE

The Mistakes That Make Us—that's a good title for a book. But I could be wrong. Have I made a mistake? Only time will tell.

- The mistakes that make us learn are ones to cherish.

- The mistakes that make us upset are opportunities to reflect on being more kind.

- The mistakes that make us examine our actions then help us improve.

- The mistakes that make us frustrated, because we've made them before, can inspire us to finally take action and improve.

- The mistakes that make us notice a small problem early on help us avoid big mistakes and possibly catastrophic failures.

- The mistakes that make us embarrassed are, hopefully, made in a workplace that chooses kindness and learning instead of blame and punishment.

- The mistakes that make us laugh brighten our day.

We can be thankful for mistakes.

HOW IT STARTED

How did this book come to be? In May 2020, a public-relations person sent an email that said, "I'm writing to introduce one of the original 'sharks' on the hit TV show *Shark Tank*, the creator of the infomercial, and pioneer of the "As Seen on TV" industry, Kevin Harrington, and his mentee, serial entrepreneur Mark Timm."

The email concluded, "I hope you'll consider an interview with Kevin and Mark on your show." Wow! Yes! I wanted to. But Kevin and Mark, and their book about mentoring, didn't tightly fit the theme of the podcast I have hosted since 2006 called *Lean Blog Interviews*.

I've been a student of "Lean Management," based on the famed Toyota Production System, applying those methods and mindsets in settings including manufacturing, healthcare, and software organizations. Toyota has long cultivated a culture of preventing mistakes and learning from them. You'll read stories in the book from Toyota people who have kept that culture alive and growing. Toyota's not perfect, but they offer us much to love and learn.

In one of my earlier books, *Practicing Lean*, fifteen authors and I shared mistakes we made early in our careers. I also wanted to change my habit of writing occasional snarky blog posts that criticized mistake-makers, implying they should have known better. As book contributors, we aimed to reassure others (and remind ourselves) that we all make mistakes when learning and doing new things. I like to think I've mended my ways. I could be wrong.

FINDING A WAY TO SAY "YES"

Thankfully, a voice in my head said, "Find a way to say *Yes*." So, I asked the PR professionals what they thought about possible themes and titles for a new business podcast. These included "My Favorite Mistake," where I proposed that guests tell a story about a mistake that turned out to be a great learning opportunity, one they wouldn't have expected at the time.

Proposing this wasn't risky. If I didn't try, I would likely regret that more. I managed to turn a potentially lost opportunity into a big one—and was delighted when Kevin and Mark said they were happy to talk about mistakes! The podcast was born!

But one episode does not a podcast make. I assumed I could find other successful people willing to open up publicly to some random guy and his podcast listeners. I assumed guests would have compelling stories to tell. If guests wanted to share only humble-brag mistakes like "I've worked too hard and been too successful," I would have chosen to scrub the podcast's launch.

Thankfully, my assumptions turned out to be true. I found guests willing not only to share vulnerable stories but also to reveal what they learned and how they adjusted—and how the pain caused by their mistake subsided with reflection over time. That allowed us to talk about making something positive out of our mistakes—and how others have done the same.

I've released more than 200 episodes to date, with more to come. I haven't tired of asking about favorite mistakes or hearing how people answer.

WHAT MAKES A MISTAKE A FAVORITE?

What's a mistake? We'll discuss that in Chapter One. What makes somebody decide that a mistake is a favorite? My question to guests is intentionally open-ended, and the answer is completely subjective. A favorite mistake is not necessarily the same as one's "biggest." Asking about people's *worst* mistakes might trigger regret and sadness.

Through these conversations, I better understood what "favorite mistake" means to a wide range of people. A favorite might be one or more of the following:

- A mistake that's important enough to stick with you

- A mistake that created a fortuitous opportunity or new direction

- A mistake we hope others can avoid

- A mistake that led to learning, including the actions required to prevent repeating the mistake

WHO PLANTED THE SEED FOR THIS BOOK?

After we finished recording their episode, one of my first guests asked me, "Did you start this podcast because you're writing a book about mistakes?" My answer was a sincere "no." I was motivated at that point by curiosity, learning, and the opportunity to meet some fantastic people.

After about a hundred episodes, as patterns emerged, I realized these interviews served as "field research." These seeds started germinating as I considered writing a book about mistakes, but I don't remember which guest did the planting! Back then, it didn't seem important to remember exactly who asked. Please let me know if you're reading this and remember asking me the question. I'm very grateful, whoever you are.

CULTIVATING THE CULTURE—WHAT'S AHEAD

In this book, you'll read about companies cultivating a culture of learning from mistakes, including global manufacturers like Toyota, software companies like KaiNexus, and, perhaps surprisingly, two small whiskey distillers. The ability to learn from mistakes isn't a technology only the largest companies can afford. It's something anybody can cultivate.

After a lot of consideration and debate, I chose the word "cultivating" to start the book's subtitle. That word was a gift from my old friend Don Coon, a professional artist who created the book's cover. I use the word throughout the book instead of alternatives like "building" or "creating." To me, "building a culture" sounds too mechanical. "Creating" one sounds like a one-time event.

I don't consider myself as having a green thumb, but we can draw parallels between a garden and our culture. The word "culture" has roots in Latin, *cultus* ("care") and French, *colere* ("to till the ground").

First, leaders need to declare the intent to start cultivating the culture. As we launch a startup, we can decide what to plant and where. Or sometimes, we discover that a healthy culture has sprouted up as a result of the way people act, so we then declare our intent to consciously keep the culture growing and thriving.

The second step is analyzing and preparing the soil that provides the foundation for our culture. What figurative rocks and weeds do we need to clear? Are any leaders making the soil too acidic for anything to grow? Are they willing and able to change, or do we need to change out certain leaders to ensure that our garden will survive?

Thirdly, leaders plant the seeds for a culture of learning from mistakes by modeling behaviors like admitting mistakes to themselves and then to others. As employees start feeling safe enough to follow their lead, others will plant more seeds by admitting their mistakes.

Finally, a garden requires continued food, water, fertilizer, and sunlight. Our culture is nurtured by what we do and how we act. Food and water are represented by leaders reacting kindly and constructively to mistakes. Effective problem-solving and process improvement are the fertilizer that accelerates growth. The sunlight of transparency means sharing of mistakes, lessons learned, and improvements—because it feels safe to do so.

The first part of the book focuses on actions that start on an individual level: thinking positively about mistakes (Chapter One), admitting mistakes (Chapter Two), and being kind to yourself and others (Chapter Three). Next, we look at methods for proactively preventing mistakes (Chapter Four) while cultivating higher psychological safety levels required for employees to feel safe in speaking up (Chapter Five). The final part of the book discusses the need for leaders to react constructively to mistakes, shifting from punishment to improvement (Chapter Six), the opportunity to iterate our way to success (Chapter Seven), and some concluding examples and thoughts about starting or continuing our cultivation efforts (Chapter Eight).

Thanks for reading. I hope you don't decide that's a mistake.

Disclosures:

I have formal business relationships with some organizations that I write about in this book:

- **KaiNexus**: Since 2011, I have been a contractor, part-time employee, and investor, owning a small equity stake in the company today.

- **Value Capture**: I previously worked for them as a part-time subcontractor (as a client advisor and in a marketing role) from 2017 through 2023.

- **LeaderFactor**: They trained and certified me in their psychological-safety education, assessment, and improvement methodologies that I license for use with organizations.

CHAPTER ONE

THINK POSITIVELY

"Experience is simply the name we give our mistakes."

—OSCAR WILDE
Irish poet and playwright (1854–1900)

We all make mistakes—even sharks.

It can be hard to admit our mistakes. Sharks don't feel that burden.

But what if the shark is Kevin Harrington, who appeared on the first season of the hit TV show *Shark Tank*? He was my first guest on the *My Favorite Mistake* podcast.[1] Just as great white sharks need continual movement to breathe and live, entrepreneurs like Kevin need a continuous flow of cash to stay alive.

A serial entrepreneur, Kevin is the inventor of the modern television "As Seen on TV" infomercial, selling famous products like the George Foreman Grill and Jack LaLanne Juicers. He admits: "30 years ago, I made a big mistake. [I've] made plenty since then."

1

Kevin's company almost went under because of *his* mistake, one he was willing to admit and discuss. Some might think the Kevin Harringtons of the business world are successful because they *avoid* making mistakes. They'd be wrong. Successful people (and organizations) are better at *learning* from mistakes, and they avoid repeating them.

Thirty years ago, Kevin's business brought in $100 million a year in revenue from a dozen products. About $2 million in sales were deposited in the bank account each Monday, driven mainly by the weekend's sales.

One week started with a shock as he arrived to find his extremely distraught chief financial officer in Kevin's office. The CFO informed Kevin that the bank had held back that week's revenue. "That $2 million represented my life," said Kevin. This situation jeopardized his ability to meet payroll and buy airtime for his infomercials. He feared this would quickly make them "As Formerly Seen on TV."

Why did the bank withhold the funds? One of Kevin's twelve infomercial products had an extremely high defect rate of 30%, which led to a flood of customer complaints and refunds. The bank held the $2 million to protect itself from the risk of potentially paying additional refunds.

At the time, Kevin's company ran the credit-card payments for all its products through a single credit-card processing account. He didn't realize this was risky until it became a huge concern. The problematic product represented just 3% of his sales, yet it put the whole company at risk.

He worked with the bank to release 80% of those funds, relieving the cash-flow pressure in the short term. Once the crisis passed, Kevin wondered if this would happen again. Would the bank be as cooperative the next time? "It's something we never wanted to go through again," he recalled.

They could stop selling the product until they could eliminate quality problems at the factory or find a new supplier. But what would they do if they had a quality problem with another product in the future? Kevin took actions to address the systemic cash-flow risk, explaining, "We set up separate accounts for every product. Separate businesses, separate profit-and-loss statements. And we ran our business completely in these little silos," which isolated the risk created by a single defective product. If complaints spiked for one product, the remaining cash flow would continue through separate accounts.

Kevin calls this his "favorite mistake" because he learned, adjusted, and prevented that mistake from happening again, describing this experience as "an amazing learning curve." He survived and grew the business to more than $500 million in annual revenue before selling the company and moving on to the new world of online advertising and sales.

Kevin also emphasizes the need to iterate when they tried launching new products, realizing "not everything was going to be a hit." The company usually tried up to three times before declaring a product dead, aiming to "fail cheap" by putting as little money as possible into the failures. Small tests of change and the benefits of iterating your way to success are discussed in Chapter Seven.

When people like Kevin publicly admit mistakes, their story could help somebody else avoid his mistake, but few of us will ever face that exact situation. However, his attitude about admitting and learning from mistakes can help us all. Creating a public persona of perfection might be tempting, but what can other people learn from that? To be perfect? To try harder to be perfect? Nah, that's not going to happen. It's not that simple.

We're more likely to learn, improve, and grow when we admit our mistakes, even if just to ourselves. Some people might succeed despite never admitting a mistake, but it's unlikely they've avoided making them. I'm positive I make mistakes every day. But I work to turn those mistakes into something positive, helping me grow, learn, and improve.

WHAT ARE MISTAKES?

Mistakes are actions or judgments that turn out to be misguided or wrong. We believe we are making the right decision at the time but eventually discover it was wrong, whether seconds or years later. The word "mistake" is a noun. Mistakes exist, whether we recognize and admit them or not. After discovering a mistake, our choices determine if we turn it into something positive (learning and improving) or make things worse (dooming ourselves to repeating them).

Mistakes arise from decisions and actions that produce outcomes that don't match our intended results. Or we decided to maintain the status quo when we should have made a change—perhaps any change. We call this an "inaction mistake."

We use the term "planning mistakes" for decisions and actions that were intentional and end up being wrong. An example was when I emailed a new colleague and typed "Kayleigh" as part of the email address, an intentional spelling choice. I quickly discovered my mistake when the email bounced back because the address did not exist. I didn't know how to spell her name correctly and made a bad assumption.

The term "execution mistakes" applies when our intended actions *would* have been correct, but we failed to follow our plan for some reason. In reply to a later email from this new employee, my fingers still managed to type "Hi, Kayleigh," even though I had already learned that her name was spelled "Kaleigh." I slipped up. We sometimes call this "human error." I quickly learned and created the habit of using her spelling, although I might make that mistake again. Sorry, Kaleigh.

We can also define a mistake as "an error in action, calculation, opinion, or judgment caused by poor reasoning, carelessness, insufficient knowledge, assumptions, etc." That definition also includes common causes of mistakes.

When we lack knowledge, we tend to fill that gap with assumptions that could be incorrect—leading to mistakes. Ideally, we could delay our decision until we get better information. If the information doesn't exist, we might need to move forward without realizing that we should test and evaluate our assumptions, ready to be proven wrong. Stubbornly clinging to assumptions can cause many mistakes. When an assumption turns out to be untrue, we must detect it early to adjust accordingly—celebrating what we learned instead of beating ourselves up (and hopefully others will react kindly). Mistakes caused by what seems like "carelessness" are usually more complicated than that. It's not that people don't *care*—even the *most* careful of us get tripped up by a badly designed process. Many types of human error can be prevented by various mistake-proofing techniques, as we'll learn about in Chapter Four.

REPLACE PUNISHMENT WITH IMPROVEMENT

Leaders and organizations have a choice: cultivate a culture of fear and punishment or a culture of learning and innovation. That choice significantly affects happiness and performance at all levels within the organization. We're better off choosing to be positive about mistakes. We don't have to love that mistakes happen. But they're a fact. Taking the positive post-mistake path leads to better outcomes over time, even if it seems like the road less traveled. More than 200 podcast guests have made that clear.

A culture of fear and punishment drives mistakes underground. An organization with a culture of fear cannot learn from mistakes, because people don't feel safe admitting them. People who *do* admit mistakes to their manager aren't more virtuous or courageous; they likely are in circumstances where they are able to feel safe doing so. Instead of telling people to be brave, leaders must help people feel safer.

Those who fail to learn from mistakes are doomed to repeat them.

A culture of learning from mistakes is kind and constructive. It's more effective. It allows people to take an active role in preventing mistakes from being repeated. In doing so, they learn how to reduce the number made over time. They feel safer and more capable of driving improvement and innovation.

Most organizations today are closer to a culture of fear and punishment than a culture of learning—it's been the corporate-culture default for a long time. Choosing to be positive and constructive about mistakes can be a differentiating competitive advantage. It will help you attract and retain top talent, and more effectively serve customers. More learning leads to more innovation, growth, and better long-term business performance.

Punishment is a hard habit to break. But we must. Lucian Leape, MD, one of the leaders of the modern patient-safety movement, reinforced this notion in testimony to Congress, making a statement that applies to most workplaces: "The single greatest impediment to error prevention in the medical industry is that we punish people for making mistakes."

Donald Berwick, MD, MPP, is president emeritus and senior fellow at the Institute for Healthcare Improvement and a former Centers for Medicare & Medicaid Services administrator. Berwick has long championed a positive view of problems. In a 1989 *New England Journal of Medicine* editorial, he cited an epigram: "Every defect is a treasure," adding, "In the discovery of imperfection lies the chance for processes to improve."[2]

Berwick said organizations could not eliminate quality problems by blaming people and removing so-called "bad apples," a lesson he learned from the best manufacturers, including Toyota. Most problems and mistakes have systemic causes, and we can discover that by asking, "How could that occur?" instead of "Whose fault is that?" The existence of a mistake does not mean that somebody messed up. Blame the process, not the people.

Many healthcare organizations use surveys, including one from Press Ganey, to ask staff members how much they agree with the following statement: "I can report patient-safety mistakes without fear of punishment."[3] In any workplace, everybody should have the ability to report mistakes of any kind without fear of punishment.

The next statement in the Press Ganey survey emphasizes the need to combine a nonpunitive approach with effective problem-solving: "In my work unit/department, we discuss ways to prevent errors from happening again." Talking must lead to action as we test and evaluate the effectiveness of our prevention efforts.

Companies in a wide range of industries choose to think positively about mistakes. It might seem easier when the consequences aren't a matter of life or death. For example, Kevin Goldsmith, chief technology officer at DistroKid, the world's largest digital-music distributor, says: "Figuring out how to fail effectively is a superpower at organizations, versus others that . . . are still punishing failure. It really destroys all innovation."[4]

A culture of learning from mistakes brings many benefits, including higher employee engagement, lower turnover, more improvement, and greater innovation. It's about better results—as individuals, teams, and organizations.

FAIL OFTEN—OR LEARN TO SUCCEED?

In recent years, entrepreneurs have been increasingly keen to talk about failures. People in Silicon Valley and other innovation centers organize "failure nights," sometimes called "F-Up Nights" (more often by the vulgar version of that phrase). Others share "failure resumes" online.

The word "failure" is sometimes used interchangeably with the word "mistake." The words are related but different. Mistakes *might lead* to failures, but failures aren't always caused by a mistake.

Mistakes are inevitable, but failure is not.

A mistake is a bad decision or an unintended slip. Failure is an outcome. When defined as "a lack of success," "failure" sounds absolute, as it implies "complete failure." If a decision leads to results falling just a little short of expectations, the word "failure" seems too harsh.

Innovators love phrases like "Fail early, fail often." I'd rather say (and experience) things like:

- Fail early, not repeatedly

- Fail fast, learn often

- Fail early, succeed later

- Fail small, not big

Let's shift the thinking from "Fail early, fail often" to "Make small mistakes early, learn, adjust, and succeed." Or, more succinctly, *small mistakes lead to success.*

Even if you're not a startup CEO, you can embrace mistakes, regardless of your profession, industry, or company size. You can foster this mindset as an individual, even if your team or other leaders in your organization do not. But it's better when your leaders share this view. If you're a leader, thinking positively plants the seeds for others to do the same.

DISCOVER GAPS BETWEEN EXPECTATIONS AND RESULTS

I've met many former Toyota employees who define a problem as "the gap between expected and actual outcomes." It can be the gap between our goal and actual levels of performance. The role of a leader is to help everyone work together to close those gaps.

Since a mistake is one type of problem, it leads me to use similar language: A mistake results in a gap between expected and actual outcomes.

Many podcast guests shared personal stories about the gap between what they expected from a new job (something positive) and the actual outcome (a bad situation). Some gaps were huge, meaning they needed to leave that job. Other gaps were relatively small, and they could be solved by staying and making the best of the mistake.

Scott Hirsch, the chief technology officer of a Canadian company, Talent Marketplace, launched the beta version of a job-search platform with a price he thought would be attractive: free. He quickly discovered the gap between his expected outcome (that many people would sign up because it was free) and the actual outcome (people were skeptical and didn't sign up). A free site seemed too good to be true. Scott learned from the early mistake, started charging customers, and began to grow.[5]

Sometimes, we can quantify the gaps. In 2015, when Kevin Goldsmith was a technology leader at Spotify, the company planned to launch a new set of features called "Spotify Now." There was a sense of urgency, as they wanted to preempt Apple's expected announcement of their music-streaming service. Spotify didn't specifically predict how much Spotify Now would boost user retention, but a modest increase of 1% would have been a "huge deal at Spotify's scale," Kevin says.

Rolling out Spotify Now to all users would risk a public failure, so they tested it by giving the features to a small group of users in New Zealand. Customers were not being charged for the Spotify Now features whether they used the free version of the Spotify service (with ads) or the paid, ad-free version. The results of the test showed a 6% increase in retention. Kevin thought those results were "amazing" but "completely unrealistic."

Based on the test results, and even with Kevin's concern about them, Spotify moved forward. They ran a slightly larger test by giving the Spotify Now features to 1% of their customers in Spotify's four largest markets. So how did it work out in the larger test? They were surprised to see a 1% *decline* in user retention. What happened?

After some investigation and further testing, Spotify learned they had inadvertently removed ads for users in this test group who used the free version. They were essentially getting the paid service for free, and that's why the test group was so happy! In this case, free was better, which distorted the results of the test and caused Spotify to draw an incorrect conclusion about the effectiveness of Spotify Now. One mistake (removing the ads for free users) led to another: deciding to move forward beyond the initial test group based on those misleading test-group results.

The 1% decline in user retention in the broader test group made the mistakes painfully clear. The gap was large enough that the word "failure" applies, as Kevin labeled it.[6] Gradually, Kevin and his team figured out which of the Spotify Now features were driving users away. After removing those and making improvements, the global rollout commenced with "a more modest retention gain," as they would have hoped.

Kevin wrote, "To Spotify's immense credit, rather than punish me, my peers, and the team, we were rewarded for how we handled the failure. The lessons we learned from the mistakes of Spotify Now were immensely beneficial to the company."[7]

As he told me, "Spotify was very good about handling failure, and I learned a lot from the company about how they handled mistakes." When leaders punish people for mistakes, they might say they are "holding people accountable," but that's often a polite way of describing punishment. As Kevin recalled, accountability was different at Spotify, adding, "You still hold people accountable, but you hold them accountable for failing well. That means if I make a mistake, I learn from it."[8]

We risk making mistakes when we create or innovate, or any time we try to improve a product, service, or process. The German word (a very long one, of course) *verschlimmbesserung* means "an attempted improvement that only worsens things." When it's safe to admit we've made it worse, we can reverse the change or make adjustments in a new attempt to make things better.

CHERISH MISTAKES

"Cherish" might seem like a strangely positive word to use regarding mistakes. Two of my podcast guests used that word, which has stuck with me since. To "cherish" a mistake means holding it dear because it's meaningful. Instead of celebrating mistakes, the gentler language of *embracing* and *cherishing* our mistakes might be closer to the truth.

The first to use the word with me in the podcast was Greg Cote, a longtime sports columnist with the *Miami Herald*, who reacted to my "favorite mistake" question by saying, "What an odd phrase. It's an oxymoron. Why would I consider a mistake to be something cherished and favorited?"

In 1982, then a reporter for the paper, Greg covered a professional soccer team in Fort Lauderdale. Greg interviewed a player from England, Ken Fogarty, in which Ken said his sister was in the British Navy, heading to fight in the Falklands War. Greg wrote an article about this for the paper.

Greg was chagrined to learn that the footballer was lying. "It was sort of embarrassing at the time, but it taught me a lesson," to double-check everything, and that's why it's Greg's favorite mistake.[9]

The word "cherish" was also used by Matt Boos, now the chief insights officer at a data-services provider, Calligo. He "cherishes" his favorite mistake because he "thinks about it every day." Earlier in his career at a major American telecommunications provider, Matt failed to ask his senior vice president for help when one of his projects was way behind schedule.

Matt was summoned to the VP's office and thought he was about to get fired. Instead, he was asked a calm-but-pointed question, "Why don't you think I deserve the honor and respect of the truth?"

The VP chose to coach and not punish. He encouraged Matt to come forward with problems, as the leader made it clear he was willing (and able) to help.[10] The lesson stuck with Matt as an employee and leader. Leaders can encourage people to speak up about bad news or problems. More importantly, they must demonstrate that it's safe to do so, as discussed in Chapter Six.

SHARING MISTAKES REQUIRES PSYCHOLOGICAL SAFETY

Using mistakes to learn and improve requires that we hear about them. But leaders can't just tell people to speak up. Telling them "It's safe" doesn't make it true. Each individual decides if they feel a level of psychological safety high enough that the potential rewards of speaking up outweigh the perceived risks.

As Harvard professor Amy Edmondson, PhD, defines in her excellent book *The Fearless Organization*:

"Psychological safety is a belief that one will not be punished or humiliated for speaking up with:

- Ideas

- Questions

- Concerns or

- Mistakes."

Leaders can't generally declare, "We are a psychologically safe organization." That's for each person to decide. The real question is, "How safe does each person feel?" Organizations that learn from mistakes share an important cultural attribute. Their culture, the way leaders behave, helps people decide if they feel safe speaking up about mistakes, as discussed in Chapter Five.

The connections are clear. Leaders who openly share their mistakes create an environment where others feel safe and willing to do the same. When an employee admits a mistake, they quickly learn how well their organization tolerates it or, better yet, welcomes it. Does their leader punish or thank them for speaking up? When their candor is rewarded by receiving help instead of abuse, this enables people to admit more mistakes, which leads to more learning and better performance.

Using the word "reward" might seem strange in the context of a mistake. That doesn't mean paying a cash bonus for making or finding mistakes. Leaders must reward the act of speaking up or, at the very least, avoid actions that appear to be punitive.

Words like "embrace" or "cherish" strike a better tone. We can embrace the person (figuratively, perhaps) and remind them we know the mistake was, by definition, unintentional. We can react in kind and constructive ways. Most likely, an employee involved in a mistake already feels terrible. Employees deserve kindness and empathy whether the mistake was an unintended "slip" or an intentional decision that turned out to be a mistake.

SHIFT AWAY FROM PUNISHMENT TO A POSITIVE PATH

Not all mistakes are created equally. Some mistakes cause more harm or damage than others. But the amount of harm is not the criterion we should use to decide if punishment is fair or warranted. See more about the "Just Culture" methodology in Chapter Six.

In some companies and circumstances, we can celebrate mistakes as an opportunity to learn and improve, even when there is a significant financial loss. In other situations, we must work diligently to prevent mistakes that cause harm and death. In part, we can prevent major mistakes by learning from small mistakes (or close calls) of the same variety that do not cause harm. Aviation does this exceedingly well. Healthcare generally does not, as discussed more in Chapter Five.

Edmondson distinguishes between three types of mistakes: *preventable, complex,* and *intelligent*. In situations where people are doing novel and innovative things, leaders can welcome intelligent mistakes, if not celebrate them, as discussed in Chapter Seven. Some mistakes are completely preventable in known ways if people are able to follow their standard process. Organizations can prevent many mistakes through approaches like checklists and other forms of mistake-proofing, as discussed in Chapter Four.

An example of a complex mistake might be a bad surgical outcome resulting from an unforeseen combination of events, leading to an unexpected mistake. In healthcare, preventable mistakes can be fatal, like performing a surgical procedure on the wrong patient or giving the wrong medication. Edmondson says, "Neither preventable nor complex failures are worthy of celebration."[11]

In truth, systemic factors cause most mistakes. If we attribute a mistake to simple human error, we wouldn't shrug it off and say, "Well, we're all human; we all make mistakes. What more can we do?" We do the right things. We don't punish. Instead, we choose to be kind and constructive. Actually, kindness *is* constructive, as discussed further in Chapter Three. We must learn from our mistakes and improve.

Firing a person for a mistake without addressing the systemic causes, especially those factors out of their control, dooms their replacement to the same mistake. Thomas J. Watson, the founder of IBM, was asked if he would "fire an employee who made a mistake that cost the company $600,000." He replied, "No, I just spent $600,000 training [them]." Watson wanted IBM to benefit from that investment, owning those lessons learned instead of letting another company hire away that experience and knowledge.

When we stop punishing people for mistakes, we start a virtuous cycle of increased learning and psychological safety. We don't do it to be nice; the goals are fewer mistakes and better business results.

IDENTIFY MISTAKES TO REFLECT, LEARN, AND IMPROVE

Brook Ward is President and CEO of Washington Health System, located southwest of Pittsburgh. He makes it a habit, whenever discovering a mistake, to ask with a positive tone: "What have we learned?"

To ensure the ensuing discussions are constructive, Brook reminds his organization that "most mistakes are due to systems issues"—bad processes, not bad people. He says this approach helps cultivate an organizational culture where "the team can learn, improve, and not be afraid of mistakes." Brook encourages groups to discuss mistakes, not as a warning for others to be careful, but so they can spread and benefit from actions taken to prevent recurrence. You'll read more about Brook and his organization's culture in Chapter Seven.[12]

When reflecting on a mistake, we can ask additional questions that I learned from the team at Value Capture, a healthcare-advisory firm:

- What decision did I make?

- What did I expect to happen?

- What actually happened?

- What did I learn from the gap?

- What would I do differently?

- What would I expect to happen?

Answering those questions helps us focus on learning from mistakes instead of shaming ourselves or others for them.

TOYOTA'S CULTURE OF LEARNING FROM MISTAKES

Isao Yoshino, who retired after 40 years in leadership roles at Toyota, the world's largest automaker, says, "The only secret to Toyota is its attitude toward learning. We don't even notice and take it for granted."

According to Yoshino, Toyota has a culture of patiently "reflecting, learning, adjusting, and continuing to try until they succeed. They are willing to experiment and embrace failure and bad news as possible sources of learning."[13]

I've worked with many people who don't like the word "problem" because it seems negative. Some people feel the same way about the word "mistake." But with the right kind of leadership, we can turn the negative into a positive. Instead of sugarcoating the situation by choosing softer words, we can lean into problems and mistakes—recognizing that the problems exist whether we like admitting them or not.

Toyota people often say, "No problems is a problem." Having no problems is a problem because it means you don't understand your business or are not admitting the truth. Toyota leaders realize that they must make it psychologically safe enough for people to reveal problems and mistakes, and they work hard to cultivate that culture.

Toyota leaders do this by visiting a site and asking questions like, "What are your top-three problems right now?" They're asking about priorities, but that question assumes problems exist, which permits others to acknowledge and discuss them. In other workplaces, asking a closed-ended question such as "Do you have any problems right now?" might lead to a quick "No" response, especially if leaders haven't proven they can react constructively when somebody answers "Yes."

When driving their first American import model, the 1955 Toyopet Crown, Shoichiro Toyoda recalled it was "dangerous to enter a highway on an uphill slope." He admitted the Crown had poor acceleration and was chagrined to realize that Toyota had exported cars to America without performing enough driving tests. He said, "After reflecting on it, we decided to give up export for the time being."[14] Toyota's first minivan, the 1991 Previa, was a flop for reasons including the presence of only two cup holders, which was not nearly enough to please American buyers. Instead of giving up, Toyota learned, adjusted, and improved. Its second-generation minivan, the Sienna, had *fourteen* cup holders.[15] Toyota continued iterating (and adding four more cup holders) and, by 2019, had surpassed Honda as the top-selling minivan in the United States.

Toyota's management system and its culture helped them become the world's largest automaker, setting a new standard for quality and productivity that drove other global automakers to eventually try copying their practices. Non-automotive manufacturers learned from and emulated Toyota, and their influence extended to companies in healthcare, software, and different service settings.

I'm not saying Toyota is perfect. No company or person is. I would cringe if a leader somewhere in that vast company chastised a team member for making a mistake today. Punishment should be the exception at Toyota, based on the company's stated values and practices. But, sadly, it's the norm in most workplaces.

Toyota employees have learned to expect a constructive and non-punitive reaction when they make or admit a mistake. If the actual response is ever some form of punishment, that would be a surprise and a problem—a gap and a mistake. I've heard enough stories from former Toyota employees that reinforce the perception of a common and consistent culture that Toyota has cultivated across continents and decades.

YOUNGER COMPANIES CAN CULTIVATE THIS CULTURE

Entrepreneur Joel Trammell, most recently founder and chairman of Khorus Systems, a strategy-execution software provider, tells CEOs, "Anytime somebody brings a problem to you, the first words out of your mouth need to be 'Thank you. Thank you for letting me know that we had a problem. Now let's talk about how we're going to solve it.'"[16]

When leaders react constructively, Joel finds that employees will "start bringing you more and more problems. And they bring you problems when they're small fires instead of after they've blown up, when there's no way to solve the problem."

Our organizational culture is like a garden. To have lasting and thriving plants or crops, our cultivation efforts can't be a one-time project; it's an ongoing effort. If you work for a large company with a long history of rocks, weeds, and poison in the soil, it's incredibly difficult to change the culture. A leader might be able to do so in their local department, with a budding garden and learning from mistakes. But that brings the risk of an executive swooping in and destroying the crops by punishing mistakes.

It's easier to cultivate a culture of learning from mistakes in smaller companies, especially when that's the clear intent from the beginning, as it was at Garrison Brothers Distillery (founded in 2005). You'll learn more about the Garrison Brothers culture in Chapter Two. Another company with this culture is KaiNexus, a small-but-fast-growing Texas-based software company (founded in 2009). Co-founder and chief operating officer Matt Paliulis says, "KaiNexus hasn't made any major mistakes, at least any existential ones. But we make a lot of little mistakes and learn, and that is why we are thriving."

Psychological safety doesn't just appear. Leaders at KaiNexus very often, and very visibly, behave in ways that create the conditions for employees to decide they can feel safe speaking up. In some settings, admitting a mistake can feel risky, if not dangerous, if people think leaders will punish them. But leaders can create conditions where that risk seems very low or non-existent. When leaders admit mistakes, with a focus on learning, that's the first step in cultivating psychological safety.

The second step is rewarding and not punishing employees who do the same.

One of those leaders is Chris Burnham, the senior director of lean strategy at KaiNexus. During a biannual meeting, Chris candidly told the entire company, "I made mistakes." He reviewed what had gone well in the first half of the year and what had gone wrong—a standard that everybody follows in giving updates.

Chris explained his mistakes, what he learned, and how he planned to adjust—a decidedly positive view of mistakes. Chris told me, "I make mistakes every day, some big, some small. But I own them all. Mistakes are how I learn and gain experience." Chris believes his transparency helps his teammates feel comfortable bringing him problems they can solve together.

While leading a team, Chris is able to follow the lead of Matt and other senior leaders, including CEO and co-founder Greg Jacobson, MD. They all admit mistakes. They nourish the culture by reacting to mistakes with the intent to learn and improve. Throughout this book, you'll read more stories illustrating the culture at KaiNexus and how they're not just reacting kindly and constructively to mistakes but also working to prevent them.

Positive thinking starts with the way we react to our own mistakes. Leaders can then extend their focus toward helping others and cultivating the culture. It's not a matter of being nice; it's about being positively helpful.

CHAPTER TWO

ADMIT MISTAKES

"To make mistakes is human; to stumble is commonplace;
to be able to laugh at yourself is maturity."

—WILLIAM ARTHUR WARD
American author (1921–1994)

Retired U.S. Representative Will Hurd was elected to Congress from Texas in 2014, winning re-election twice before stepping down in 2020.

He lost his first campaign. Because of his mistake.

Will is, by most measures, one of the most consistently successful people I've ever met. He was elected student-body president at Texas A&M, stepping up as a leader with national prominence after mistakes (not his) led to the tragic collapse of a bonfire that killed 12 people. Will served as an undercover officer for the CIA in Afghanistan after 9/11, where a mistake could have gotten himself or others killed.

In 2010, when Will first ran for Congress, he received the most votes in his party's primary for the 23rd district. He bested four candidates, including the frontrunner who'd previously held that seat. However, the contest went to a runoff because he didn't get 50% of the vote.

He lost the runoff by 700 votes.

Why? Will admits he didn't listen to his political consultants, who told him that a runoff is an entirely different type of election, requiring different tactics and strategies. Will insisted on continuing the strategy that got him the most votes, treating the runoff as "a continuation of the first election."[17]

For the runoff, Will assumed that continuing the same strategy would lead to victory. His consultants thought he was making a mistake, which was confirmed when they saw the election-day results. While other candidates might have blamed the consultants for not being convincing enough with their advice, Will didn't blame bad data. He took ownership of his strategic and tactical mistakes instead.

It's not exactly news that politicians make mistakes, but it's surprising to hear one admit it. Will says, "I think we learn most from our mistakes," adding, "If I'd known in advance [it was a mistake], I wouldn't have done it." Will wasn't sabotaging his campaign; the decision he thought to be correct turned out to be wrong.

When Will ran again in 2014, he built the campaign organization differently. "We weren't going to make the same mistake," he recalls. The second time, his entire organization focused on ensuring those who voted for him in the first primary election were convinced to return and vote in the runoff, this time following the advice his consultants gave him in 2010.

Admit Mistakes

After winning re-election twice, Will chose not to run again in 2020, returning to the private sector, where the habits of admitting and owning mistakes will continue to serve him well as a leader.

Was it a mistake for Will to leave Congress? Only time will tell. And perhaps only he can decide. He has a long career ahead and will make more mistakes. He sets a great example for us by:

- Admitting his mistakes

- Owning them

- Learning from them

- Adjusting in a way that leads to better results the second time

In Chapter Five, we'll hear the story of another member of Congress who reacted constructively to a staffer's mistake.

GET MORE COMFORTABLE ADMITTING MISTAKES

When I realize I've made a mistake, I start by admitting it to myself. It helps me to use phrases like:

- My mistake

- That was a mistake

- I made a mistake

In the past year, I've tried to say those words aloud as often as possible, which happens at least a few times a day. And those are just the mistakes I notice. For me, acknowledging a mistake reduces some of the emotion involved. Calling them out normalizes that mistakes happen, and we all make them, which helps me stay positive about moving forward better.

Over time, I've tried to get less upset about small mistakes. I can shrug off small ones more easily, like a minor slip-up with little impact. When it's a significant mistake, I try to remind myself to take a breath and keep calm, reminding myself that we all make mistakes and that it's an opportunity to recover, learn, and improve. That's often easier said than done, as the "fight or flight" reaction is more of a human instinct than a choice.

I'm willing to admit to making many mistakes in producing and hosting *My Favorite Mistake* and other podcasts, as I discussed in episode 200.[18] In 2021, I tried a new web-based podcasting app that promised better recordings than Zoom. That was true, except for occasional glitches. Also frustrating was that the web tool required me to provide detailed instructions to guests when this wasn't needed with Zoom, thanks to its pandemic popularity.

While the video resolution from the web-based system was much better, as promised, the two separate tracks (for the guest and me) were often out of sync, a problem I had never encountered with Zoom. This problem created the need for time-consuming editing. I eventually admitted the mistake and went back to Zoom. I had a reasonably strong hypothesis that the change would be an improvement, but it turned out to be wrong. That's OK. I learned. I adjusted.

Kurt Wilkin, an entrepreneur and investor, calls himself a "proud mistake-maker" in his bio. I love it. Kurt says, "I believe we learn best from our own experiences, and definitely from our mistakes—if we have the right attitude. I like to say the bigger the shitshow, the bigger the lesson I'm going to learn." He adds, "If we only look at our successes and pat ourselves on the back, we're never going to get better."[19]

I make mistakes and am OK with that. When successful people admit mistakes, they help us feel better about ourselves. They made mistakes and are still thriving, demonstrating that we can make mistakes and still flourish, as long as we learn and improve.

FIGHT THE TENDENCY TO HIDE MISTAKES

It's normal for us to want to hide mistakes. On one level, we might feel embarrassed. In a group setting, we might fear being ridiculed or punished (which, alas, is a real fear in many workplaces).

Amantha Imber, PhD, is an Australian organizational psychologist and founder of the behavioral-science consultancy Inventium. Her favorite mistake was a pattern of connecting her self-worth to her accomplishments. She used to think talking about her achievements would make her more likable. Amantha feared that people would think less of her if she admitted failures and mistakes.[20] She learned that was a mistaken belief.

Amantha says, "Talking about being vulnerable as a leader has become a bit of an overused cliché. But there is something very important about being open and human with your team. It makes you more effective as a leader."

It's often difficult to admit mistakes to ourselves and in relatively low-risk settings with friends. We can work on that, starting with being kinder to ourselves. But it's easier to be more open about mistakes when we work for leaders who help us learn from mistakes, instead of punishing us for them.

LIFT THE BURDEN BY TALKING ABOUT REGRETS AND MISTAKES

Daniel H. Pink is the author of bestselling books, including his most recent, *The Power of Regret*. Mistakes are one cause of regrets. Dan's favorite mistake, by the way, was a pattern of inaction. In his fifties, Dan realized he had never had a mentor and hadn't fully considered the impact of not having one.

Dan says to stop worrying that others think less of us for admitting something vulnerable, like a mistake. Research shows people "admire our candor, empathize with us, and admire our courage," he explains.

Dan says it's very helpful to talk about regrets. Why? Doing so "lifts the burden" by turning something amorphous into concrete words, as spoken or written and "the words are less frightening than the amorphous thoughts."

Dan articulates the benefits of sharing mistakes, saying, "You normalize it, you neutralize it." To help extract a lesson from a mistake, it helps to distance yourself based on the idea that "we're much better at solving other people's problems than our own."[21] As leaders become more comfortable admitting mistakes to themselves and others, they can start cultivating a culture that allows their employees to do the same.

IS IT SAFE TO ADMIT YOUR MISTAKES RIGHT NOW?

When deciding whether to admit a mistake to others, we need to consider the risk/reward ratio. How much do we risk by admitting a mistake in a particular setting and situation? While I admire those who share mistakes (in a workplace or a podcast), they have each decided it's safe (or safe enough) to do so. They might feel like they have nothing to lose or are in a privileged position that would allow them to absorb or bounce back from any reputational hit they might fear.

Even though people *generally* think more highly of those who admit mistakes, that doesn't mean your manager or organization would feel the same. Deciding when to share a mistake is an individual and situational decision. I'm not saying you *should* admit mistakes regardless of your situation or circumstances. It's not always safe to do so.

If you *know* (or strongly suspect) you would be punished or harmed by admitting a mistake, you're right to protect yourself. If that's the case, I hope you can find an organization or a situation where admitting mistakes leads to positive and constructive responses. I hope you can find a better garden or start cultivating psychological safety in a startup of your own.

CULTIVATE A CULTURE OF ADMITTING
MISTAKES, LIKE GARRISON BROTHERS

When you visit the website for Garrison Brothers Distillery, the first thing you will read under "Our Story" is the tale of the first barrels of Bourbon they tried aging in Texas heat. "The scorching heat nuked the barrels. They leaked. Cracked. Broke altogether. Hundreds of gallons were lost." Instead of giving up, founder and CEO Dan Garrison learned and adjusted. He found a cooperage willing to make "custom barrels with staves thick enough to stand up to the Texas heat."[22]

Even with early failures, they're now doing many things right. Their "Cowboy Bourbon" was twice named "U.S. Micro Whisky of the Year" by *The Jim Murray Whisky Bible.* Their "Balmorhea" Bourbon received that same recognition for three consecutive years, from 2020 to 2022, meaning Garrison Brothers won that recognition five times in seven years.

In a bit of an upset, the 2023 "U.S. Micro Whisky of the Year" was awarded to a newer Kentucky startup, Glenns Creek Distilling. You'll also read about them in Chapter Eight. Why? Because both distilleries have a culture of learning from mistakes.

Does Garrison Brothers, located in Hye, Texas (population 104), still make mistakes? Yes. And they keep admitting them. Some of those mistakes are costly, says master distiller Donnis Todd. "We've had folks stick [forklift] forks through a building and burn up a pump."[23]

Donnis reflects, "There's something about your character growing when you own up to your mistakes." That's why Donnis decided he and his team would own up to mistakes for pragmatic reasons, including fewer surprises about problems, like that burned-up pump, that could interrupt production. This practice proved to have value far beyond keeping the stills running. Donnis admits he did not have the vision to anticipate the full benefits of this approach, but he says it was one of the best things he's implemented.

Admit Mistakes

Walking around the distillery, you'll see places where employees have signed their initials to mark where mistakes occurred. People feel safe doing so because of their leaders' attitudes toward mistakes.

Donnis has a crucial leadership role, but it's important that Dan, as founder and CEO, has led the way in cultivating positive mindsets about mistakes from the beginning. Dan says, "If you screwed up, that's okay. By admitting that you're telling the company that this happened, I did it this way, and it was wrong. And you can fix it next time. And I'll be the person that will take the lead to make sure it never happens again."

Organizations like Garrison Brothers that habitually own their mistakes generally do so as a byproduct of something more important: habits of curiosity, learning, and respect for every individual.

AS A LEADER, BE FIRST TO ADMIT YOUR MISTAKES

A leader can't just tell people they should speak up about mistakes. They can't mandate that employees feel safe to do so. Leaders must model the right behaviors, including admitting mistakes and being kind to themselves and others.

Psychologist Dr. Nicole Lipkin says leaders must realize that "If you want people to be vulnerable, you need to be vulnerable," because we naturally mimic each other. Behaviors can be contagious. Nicole observes that more-vulnerable leaders are the ones with teams who feel the highest levels of psychological safety.[24]

Donnis recalls a group of 100 barrels he filled in 2015. Three and a half years later, he "absolutely loved" the taste and the quality. "I should have used those barrels right then and there, but I did not," Donnis admits.

Donnis discovered a mistake through a gap that emerged between his expected and actual outcomes. Donnis thought aging those barrels for another year or two would turn good Bourbon into something exceptional.

In oak barrels, Bourbon generally improves over the years, as it extracts more flavor from the charred-oak barrels, but some customers might complain about it tasting too "oaky" if it's been aged too long.

Another downside of aging Bourbon is the evaporative loss that occurs over time (since wood is porous and sometimes leaks). With time, the Bourbon gets better (to a point), but you know some will evaporate each year. The typical Texas summer heat means Garrison Brothers loses more of the evaporated "angel's share" each year than distillers in cooler climates like Kentucky or Scotland.

Donnis planned for that higher angel's share but was surprised by how hot the summer of 2017 turned out to be. The annual evaporative loss was three times more than usual. Each barrel would have normally yielded 50 bottles, but Donnis got, on average, only about twenty bottles from each barrel, with some producing just four or seven.

Donnis recalls, "I lost 3,000 bottles of Bourbon that I should have used in 2015. So, it hurt. It hurt financially. It hurt my pride to make such a stupid mistake." Donnis shouldn't be too hard on himself. Yes, it was an expensive mistake. Those 3,000 bottles would have sold to a distributor for $50 each or a gift-shop retail customer for $100. Therefore, the revenue loss ranged from $150,000 to $300,000.

I don't agree with Donnis' self-assessment that he was "stupid." Mistakes aren't caused by stupidity, and intelligent people make mistakes. Secondly, he was innovating, doing something others hadn't done before, aging whiskey in extreme Texas heat. When we innovate, we're going to make mistakes. Hopefully, we are allowed to learn, like Donnis.

Dan didn't punish Donnis for the loss. Their partnership has thrived for more than a decade because, as Donnis puts it, Dan "has always been willing to give me the time to learn from my mistakes. I'm truly blessed."

"He's been very, very patient with me, allowing me to make costly mistakes but to learn from them." Donnis recalls Dan took the news "about as well as anyone can" and consoled him by saying, "In time, we'll forget about the revenue loss, and we'll gain from this knowledge, to apply it, and keep making better Bourbon."

Donnis emphasized what he learned and how he adjusted. For example, he directed the coopers (barrel makers) to tweak the design of the barrels so they would stand up better to the Texas heat. Donnis learned important lessons about how to make a cask-strength single-barrel Bourbon, and it helped him improve future releases of the award-winning high-proof "Cowboy Bourbon" release.

Dan's supportive leadership allows Donnis to focus on learning and improvement. Dan adds, "At some point, we had to see how long we can age Bourbon without losing the contents of that barrel completely. And that's what we learned from it." They were "testing the boundaries of maturation," he said. Their learning is something you can taste, two ounces at a time.

Even having an understanding CEO, Donnis still felt terrible, and he put that on himself. But celebrating the value of learning helped Donnis feel better and move on. Experiments don't always work out—if they always work out as expected, they aren't really experiments.

Perhaps they could have tried learning the lesson on a smaller, less-costly scale, as discussed in Chapter Seven. Dan and Donnis can cherish the mistake for setting the distillery up for greater success because of a culture that chooses to learn instead of punishing mistake-makers.

AS A FOUNDER OR CEO, ADMIT YOUR
MISTAKES TO HELP OTHERS

The Garrison Brothers culture starts with Dan's willingness to share mistakes. One almost jeopardized his relationship with the president of Total Wine & More, the retailer that sells, by far, the most Garrison Brothers Bourbon in the United States.

One day, after hearing reports of distribution and inventory challenges at the stores, Dan fired off a heated email with a strong allegation, telling the president, "It's almost as if you're intentionally trying to crush my business." Dan referred to this email as a "stupid" mistake, as it drew an angry reply from the president. Dan managed to repair the relationship to the point where it's absolutely rock solid, with the president being a huge fan of Garrison Brothers to this day. Dan thinks the relationship is stronger because of that incident and the effort to rebuild it.

Like Donnis, Dan is not stupid. They each learn and recover from mistakes. Dan now realizes he should have just slept on it, trusting his team to sort out the situation—as it resolved itself quickly. Could he stop firing off heated emails? Knowing you should change is sometimes easier said than done.

Dan admits that he still "gets heated," especially when he hears something negative about his product, given how much he cares about his company and team. But Dan is working on controlling his emotions more often. If he hasn't learned, he is learning. We can celebrate that progress and growth.

MY UNEXPECTED OPPORTUNITY TO PUT THE GARRISON BROTHERS CULTURE TO THE TEST

After we joined the Garrison Brothers' "Old 300" club, my wife and I attended the annual "Bourbon Camp" event in September 2014. We pumped newly distilled Bourbon into a barrel that I hammered shut. Almost seven years later, we had the opportunity to taste and purchase the bottled contents.

A few weeks before our trip to the distillery, I woke up to read a shocking email from Donnis that read, "Unfortunately, while digging your barrel out of container #7, I lost control of a 600-lb. French Oak barrel that crushed your barrel. This mistake was 100% my fault, and I feel terrible."

That meant that the contents were spirited away into the porous dirt floor. Even though my wife and I were disappointed by this news, we were glad nobody got hurt. As for our barrel: Rest in Pieces.

Dan and Donnis were both apologetic, and getting upset with them wouldn't help. The financial loss was theirs, not mine, because the Bourbon was their property. Donnis could have told some tall tale, such as saying they accidentally blended it into one of their award-winning releases. To Donnis' credit, he owned up to the mistake. He was living their culture.

Dan and Donnis allowed us to taste the barrel distilled just before ours, having been aged right next to it for about seven years. That barrel tasted better than what we remembered of "ours," so we decided to become the owners of bottles with custom labels reading "ONE OFF." The serial number was one off from ours, and like any single-barrel spirit, its unique flavor will never exist again. Cheers to everybody at Garrison Brothers. I can add their culture of owning up to mistakes as something I love about their people, place, and product.

THE ACQUISITION MADE A NAME FOR THE COMPANY BUT INCLUDED A MISTAKE

Jim McCann founded a fast-growing chain of florist shops with expanding telesales operations but wanted a phone number that was easy to remember. In 1986, Jim acquired a company with the 1-800-FLOWERS phone number that later became the company name. At the time, the only way to get the phone number was to buy the corporate entity that had been assigned that number by the phone company. He couldn't simply pay to get the number re-assigned to him.[25]

In executing that brilliant move, Jim admits he didn't do enough due diligence. Referring to what he now calls his "due negligence," Jim explained he was guilty of being too cheap by not spending money on lawyers, bankers, and accountants, and thought he could do it himself. As a result, Jim acquired a failing company with $7 million in debt that became his personal liability.

Why was that Jim's favorite mistake? The high debt load forced him to hustle harder and think more broadly and grandly about growing his business more quickly. Within five years, Jim says 1-800-FLOWERS became the first national brand in the floral industry.

Jim owned—and avoided repeating—this mistake as his company grew organically and through many acquisitions. Making that mistake relatively early helped Jim learn when the cost was relatively low.

Jim cultivates a culture of recognizing, sharing, and learning from mistakes as one of the key aspects of the company's growth and success.

"It comes down to culture and leadership. They're intertwined." Jim advises that, if an employee makes a mistake while trying to do the right thing on behalf of a customer, they need to "make sure they know it's OK." He adds, "Sharing some of your [own] mistakes is the quickest and easiest way to do that."

Jim says, "We're always learning. We make mistakes but try not to make the same mistakes." He often jokes about his favorite mistake even though it was "painful for a long time."

1-800-FLOWERS.COM has a culture of sharing mistakes instead of shaming people for them. One longtime employee created what they called the "wall of shame" and put all of the "worst ideas" up on the wall, as Jim described it.

He explains, "It wasn't really shameful. It was designed to take the shame out of it because we all have things that we've done in our life that we're ashamed of. And [shame is] a powerful, crippling emotion. But when you turn it into a joke or laugh at yourself . . . it helps us to compartmentalize it. It tells the people around you that you can make mistakes but that you should try to learn from them. Try not to make the same one again, and turn it into a positive experience, a learning experience."

In 1-800-FLOWERS.COM town-hall meetings, they poke fun at mistakes, so, perhaps counterintuitively, people feel more comfortable sharing theirs. This approach might not work in every workplace, but taking a lighthearted tone when acknowledging mistakes fits their culture. To Jim, this practice strengthens the openness and safety around admitting mistakes, allowing them to learn and improve.

Even with his willingness to discuss them, Jim tries not to spend too much time thinking about any particular mistake or getting paralyzed by reflecting on them. He adds that it's important for leaders to "pick ourselves up, dust ourselves off, and get on with it."

HAVE A COACH POINT OUT MISTAKES YOU CAN'T SEE

Retired-NFL-cornerback-turned-entrepreneur Lenny Walls says football taught him a lot about how it's never "too late to change, grow, fix the situation, and bounce back" after mistakes. His mistakes were often visible to 70,000 fans in the stadium or millions on television. Because a mistake is often followed by another down 40 seconds later, he was taught to "have a short-term memory and focus on the next play."[26]

Lenny was painfully aware of many mistakes but found it helpful when coaches, from their sideline or press-box views, pointed out mistakes he didn't recognize. "We definitely wanted to correct those mistakes so they didn't continue to happen," but that sometimes had to wait until the next time he was off the field, during halftime, after the game, or during a detailed game-film review during the week between games.

VIEW MISTAKES AS AN INVESTMENT, NOT A COST

Hank Levine is the CEO of iPlace, which provides managed recruiting services for companies worldwide. He told me and an internal webinar audience of more than 400 employees, "Mistakes are very good if we use them as a learning experience. If they are a learning experience, they are not a cost. They are an investment in improvement."

He says iPlace is a "knowledge-sharing company" and "everybody is a leader" as part of their core values. As Hank explained, "Everyone here is hired because they're smart, and they have a lot of experience . . . and we all make mistakes. So as a company, we need to know that, when someone else makes mistakes on their team, we don't attack them. We talk to them. We learn from them. And we try to create an environment where we can share their learnings so that everybody can get better and every mistake is not a cost—it's an investment."

Earlier in the webinar, after my initial presentation, Hank led by example, sharing a vulnerable story about when he worked for a telecom company earlier in his career. As part of an effort to design a user interface for their new cable-TV competitor, his passion for the shortcomings in the planned UI and his confidence in the superiority of his alternative design almost got him fired. He learned that being right wasn't enough; he had to learn how to bring others along with his ideas as a leader. Sharing that story allowed his employees to feel safe sharing "favorite mistake" stories, and Hank listened attentively and thanked them for sharing their stories and lessons learned.

SHIFT FROM DEMANDING PERFECTION TO LEARNING TOGETHER

It seems relatively easy for individuals to embrace the idea that some of our best learning comes from mistakes. We hear it all the time. So why do so many organizations (which are basically collections of people) fall into the trap of creating a culture that unrealistically demands perfection, punishing even the smallest of mistakes?

Admitting and sharing mistakes is helpful but not sufficient. The sharing must be followed by a constructive response from leaders that encourages learning, action, and improvement.

Thankfully, some organizations embrace the idea of learning from mistakes. Some companies ensure that information and learning about any safety incident (or near miss) is shared globally within hours. Learning from mistakes doesn't mean we must wait to learn by repeating a mistake made elsewhere.

In some cases, entire *industries* (such as commercial aviation) share mistakes and lessons learned widely in non-punitive ways, resulting in significant economic and societal benefits. I know of isolated cases where hospitals in a region decided to share mistakes and lessons learned with other hospitals, including competitors. That's something I wish were the rule instead of the exception.

Discussing mistakes within a team means we can learn from (and support) each other. We can cultivate a learning culture by embracing mistakes as opportunities. We can look at them in a structured way to understand better how these mistakes happened in order to prevent their recurrence.

My experiences (and my podcast guests) led me to form a hypothesis that I strongly believe: All other things being equal, the company that more effectively learns from mistakes will outperform those who don't. It's a matter of culture, not character and courage.

Leaders lead the way by admitting mistakes and helping others feel safe enough to do the same, as discussed in Chapter Five. Second, being kind to themselves, as discussed in Chapter Three, helps leaders cultivate the culture by reacting constructively to the mistakes of others, as discussed in Chapter Six.

CHAPTER THREE

BE KIND

"Being kind doesn't mean being soft or a wuss. Kindness is not a sign of weakness. It is a sign of confidence . . . Taking care of employees is perhaps the best form of kindness."[27]

—COLIN POWELL

United States Secretary of State and United States Army General

(1937–2021)

"No." Lynn Yap's travel request was denied. This wasn't just any trip. Lynn wanted time off so she could visit her dying grandmother in Kuala Lumpur, having not seen her in quite some time. As an investment banker in 2012, Lynn was working 80 to 100 hours a week, proud to be part of a prestigious deal—Facebook's initial public offering.

Her team leader made it clear this wasn't up for discussion. Lynn was disappointed and feared that going would have resulted in being pulled from the project, getting a lower bonus, and perhaps being fired for not being fully committed to her work.[28]

Lynn was deeply conflicted but chose to continue working on the deal. Her grandmother died right after the IPO. Nobody at work asked about her. Lynn felt guilty and disappointed, if not angry, at herself for not standing up for her values and supporting her family.

After some time, Lynn could finally talk about her mistake. She reflected and left banking, moving forward with a strengthened sense of purpose to "not sacrifice my values . . . to value people and respect people for who they are and the value they brought to the business." Lynn now describes her favorite mistake as an opportunity for growth.

"Something I've learned over the years is the need to be kind to yourself. To grow and learn from our mistakes, we need to look back and say, 'Hey, that was OK.' The important thing is moving forward. Over time, I've learned to go easy on myself. It's OK to take more risks because it's OK to make mistakes. It's OK to fail as long as I have the courage to stand up again and take the next step."

Lynn wrote *The Altruistic Capitalist: How to Lead for Purpose and Profit* and founded Activ8 Network to increase women's participation in technology and entrepreneurship. She notes how business leaders often *say*, "People are our most important asset," but Lynn wants to create opportunities where that is actually true. She'll never tell somebody they can't travel to visit a dying family member.

Be Kind

"KIND" IS BETTER THAN "NICE"

Most people want to be nice. A nice leader, however, might avoid conflict by ignoring a mistake, or they might say, "Don't feel bad; it's not your fault." Nice might be a touch better than screaming at yourself or punishing others. But does niceness help us prevent mistakes and improve performance?

Karyn Ross, the founder of The Love and Kindness Project Foundation, co-authored *The Toyota Way to Service Excellence* and most recently wrote *The Kind Leader*.

Karyn defines kindness as "an action (or set of actions) connecting a person's internal feelings of empathy and compassion . . . that is undertaken with the purpose of generating a positive effect and outcome for another," and this also applies to yourself.[29]

She emphasizes that kindness is helpful and effective. While niceness might include qualities like sympathy and politeness (or telling people what you think they want to hear), kindness is "focused on what will help the other person learn, grow, and improve."

Her favorite mistake was losing a suitcase in Chicago's O'Hare International Airport terminal. Or maybe it was stolen. Why did this happen? What did she learn?[30] Because of chronic shoulder pain, Karyn usually checked her suitcase. One time, she kept it with her. While waiting for her flight, Karyn was increasingly annoyed by a negative work conversation. Distracted by this and being out of her regular routine, Karyn's gate was changed, and she lost track of her bag in the process. It disappeared, and she never got it back.

"The universe took my suitcase to remind me we always have a choice." Karyn says this mistake helped her realize that, when we choose to stop focusing on negative and unkind thoughts, and being frustrated by others' negativity or mistakes, we can be more present and aware in the current moment.

Karyn enjoyed the opportunity to replace her boring black suitcase, which looked like so many other travelers' bags, with one that was bright and colorful as a reminder that she could choose to be upbeat and kind.

Karyn reassured me that being kind doesn't always happen naturally for her—it's a choice. "We have a whole lifetime we've been given to practice and learn things. There are things that I've been working on since I was a child. I'm still working on them now."

Her thinking reminds me of the "growth mindset" concept, as explained in Carol Dweck's seminal book *Mindset*. With a growth mindset, we realize that we can practice kindness and get better at choosing it as an attitude or response. The "fixed mindset" alternative can be limiting because that view suggests one is inherently kind or not.

As we cultivate our ability to learn from mistakes, the growth mindset applies even better to the garden analogy. Instead of viewing ourselves as inherently good leaders (or not), a growth mindset encourages us to develop ourselves as leaders so we can cultivate others.

What is Karyn's advice for times when we make a mistake? "At that moment, when your inner voice starts [with] all those unkind things, step out for a moment and ask, 'If this happened to someone else, my friend, and they came to me and told me this, what would I say to them?' Chances are, what you're saying to yourself is not what you would say to them out loud. We have to think kindly, speak kindly, and act kindly to others, but we must [do so] to ourselves as well."

Karyn told me, "We learn self-kindness by practicing empathy, compassion, and taking kind actions for others. The best way to learn to be kind to yourself is to deliberately practice kindness to others!" She told me, "The people around us at home and work make mistakes all the time. We need not only to practice empathy and compassion but also to take action to help. Focusing on that teaches us to get out of ourselves and be kind to ourselves. We are just as imperfect."

I've learned I can be kind to myself when I realize . . . I'm being unkind to myself after a mistake. I'm not looking to make excuses for being hard on myself, but to recognize it's a pretty normal thing to do. That awareness helps me focus on choosing kindness instead of dwelling on the times when I'm not.

Karyn inspired me to create a coffee mug with four short mantras. I often drink coffee, especially when recording *My Favorite Mistake* episodes. The podcast logo faces the camera and my guest, but I see the side that reads:

- Be kind to yourself

- Nobody is perfect

- We all make mistakes

- Let's learn from our mistakes and help others do the same

The mug helps me remember these things I know to be true. I notice my mistakes, for sure. But I've gotten better at pointing out the fact of the mistake (which can be helpful) without shaming myself (which is unkind and unhelpful).

SMART PEOPLE MAKE MISTAKES

Many of my podcast guests referred to their mistakes as "dumb" or "stupid," including Donnis Todd and Dan Garrison in Chapter Two. I cringe when I hear that language in the workplace. A mistake is a fact. It exists. The adjectives we use to label our mistakes—that's a choice.

It's not "dumb" to make a decision that turns out to be wrong. If we must call anything "dumb," it would be not learning from the mistake. It's not "stupid" to slip up by clicking the wrong date while booking a hotel reservation. That's a reminder to myself because I make that mistake a lot. It's human error. None of us are perfect.

We can choose to be kind, trying to remember not to label our mistakes with derogatory terms. And if we slip up and use such language, even in our inner monologue, we can be kind to ourselves about that. Being more aware of this might help us remember not to describe other people's mistakes using such words. And we can remind others when we hear that language, directed at themselves or others, that mistake-makers are not dumb. I'd argue that intelligent people make more mistakes because they are more likely to learn and try new things, which means mistakes are inevitable.

LEARN THE SCIENCE OF HOW OUR
BRAINS REACT TO MISTAKES

We can remind ourselves to be kind and react well to mistakes, but that's easier said than done for several reasons. One reason is the wiring and evolution of our brains.

Dr. Julia DiGangi is the founder and CEO of Neuro Health Partners LLC and earned a PhD in psychology. Her neuroscience expertise is in the relationship between the brain and traumatic stress.

Julia describes the brain as a pain-detection machine, and asking it not to detect pain is like asking the lungs not to breathe. A specific part of the brain, the medial frontal cortex, recognizes mistakes. If we're alone, making simple mistakes usually doesn't bother us as much since it doesn't highly activate that part of the brain.[31] "The mistakes that bother people are always when there's some painful emotion—shame, humiliation, inadequacy, or embarrassment," she explains. The brain might start telling us we're not good enough. Then, the brain becomes "super sensitive to mistakes."

Instead of working to avoid pain, Julia says we should choose the most powerful pain, meaning the one that makes it most likely for us to learn and grow. Trying something new means making mistakes and experiencing pain. The decision *not* to try something could also bring pain. So, the most powerful pain, in her terms, is to try. When the thought of trying something new causes anxiety, she says the best way to overcome it is through exposure. "Practice does reduce anxiety."

How can we move past perfectionism, the fear of making mistakes? When trying something new that might bring emotional pain, Julia recommends starting slowly, as we might in the gym with weights. If you fear making a mistake as a public speaker, you won't leap directly to the equivalent of lifting a one-hundred-pound weight twelve times. So, we might begin by using a teleprompter or memorizing the speech. Working through a little bit of pain builds our capabilities to do better the next time, with less anxiety and pain—just as we would with weights. A personal trainer, Lenny Walls, from Chapter Two, taught me to stop putting the weights down when my muscles started shaking from fatigue. Learning to push through a few final reps is the way we actually build muscle.

When you feel the emotional pain of making a mistake, Julia hopes that, instead of saying, "I'm never doing that again," you'll ask what you can do to stretch your capabilities just slightly. In my words, *choose progress over perfection*.

SHOW KINDNESS WHEN TRYING SOMETHING NEW

After writing her book *Learning to Lead, Leading to Learn: Lessons from Toyota Leader Isao Yoshino on a Lifetime of Continuous Learning,* author and leadership coach Katie Anderson chose to record and produce her audiobook twice because of mistakes she and her team made (and didn't catch) before the initial 2021 release.[32]

Katie hired a team to produce the audiobook and spent more than 20 hours recording the first version. However, days after its release, Katie's husband discovered that the quality of a few sections wasn't up to the standard that he expected from a professional audiobook. While the sound had passed Audible's quality-control process, several sections had a lower-grade sound. Katie greatly appreciated that a handful of early listeners also kindly reached out to her about the issue personally, instead of leaving negative reviews on Audible.

Katie's heart sank when she discovered this problem, as she wanted the best listening experience for her audience. But she reassured herself knowing that, during the pandemic, she didn't have an opportunity to use a professional recording studio. She had done her best at the time, at home.

Katie had two options—accept the lower-grade chapters in the audiobook, or find a way to fix them. She immediately took action, found a recording studio, re-recorded the entire book, and released the new version.

After discovering the audiobook sound-quality problems, Katie reminded herself she was doing something new. She had carefully set up a home recording studio, hired a producer, and conducted sound-quality tests. The audio-quality problems weren't caused by a bad microphone, as she first suspected. She ultimately realized the issue was rooted in recording software that required her to click a button each time to properly connect her professional-grade microphone. She had no way of knowing if the recording quality was good while she was recording it.

"It wasn't mistake-proofed." We'll learn more about that in Chapter Four.

So, instead of beating herself up, Katie also gave herself a second chance. She found a professional studio where the producer sat outside the recording booth and monitored the quality as she read, stopping Katie as soon as some minor issue appeared. She hired audio proofreaders to pore over the entire recording for quality problems after making the mistake of doing only a few spot checks the first time.

As recounted in her book (and my podcast), her mentor and subject of her book *Learning to Lead, Leading to Learn*, Isao Yoshino, made many mistakes throughout his career. You'll read a mistake from the first year of his career in Chapter Five, which his first manager reacted to by saying, "Don't worry. Mistakes can happen. You are just a beginner, and you did your best."

Toward the end of his 40-year tenure, Yoshino led a startup boat business that failed and lost $13 million for Toyota. Bookending Yoshino's career, then-Chairman Fujio Cho told him, "You were new to the boat business. And so were we at headquarters. We all make mistakes, particularly when we try something totally new. We know you took on a challenge and worked so hard to make it happen." They reacted constructively, and that inspired Katie to do the same.

Katie released the new-and-improved audiobook six weeks after discovering problems with the first attempt. She was pleased with the result, as were new listeners, who left five-star reviews. In Katie's final reflection, she said:

"I learned a lot, but, most importantly, I'm proud of how I showed up in response to learning about a mistake and how I handled myself in dealing with my team members—looking at the process, not blaming people, even though I felt frustrated. I looked with greater reflection on the role that my actions played, the assumptions I made, and really what we could all learn going forward." Katie was kind and took action to correct her mistake.

PRACTICE SELF-COMPASSION, AND APOLOGIZE FOR YOUR MISTAKES

Kristin Neff, PhD, is the author of books including *Self-Compassion: The Proven Power of Being Kind to Yourself* and the 2021 follow-up book *Fierce Self-Compassion: How Women Can*

Harness Kindness to Speak Up, Claim Their Power, and Thrive. Holding a doctorate in Educational Psychology and Human Development, Kristin progressed from assistant professor to associate professor at the University of Texas at Austin.

Years ago, a new assistant professor refused to pass one of Kristin's dissertation students.[33] In a follow-up meeting with the student and the professor, Kristin acknowledged that the work had some issues that needed rectifying. But she felt that the professor was being too demanding and overly stringent about passing the student.

Kristin was surprised to receive an email from her department chair explaining that Kristin's admittedly passionate defense had gotten loud—her voice had carried and was overheard by many others in the department.

"I think I was a little more passionate than I had intended, especially toward a new assistant professor. I got a little carried away in defense of my student. I was kind of a 'mama bear.'"

How did she mitigate this mistake? She apologized.

At the next day's department meeting, Kristin said, "I am so sorry" to the new professor in front of the others. She continued, "I know my position of power. I really shouldn't have raised my voice. I'm sorry if I scared you. If anyone in the hall, any students, or anyone here felt at all uncomfortable, I really apologize. *Mea culpa.* I got too passionate and kind of protective over my student. Please forgive me." Her words surprised her colleagues, who weren't accustomed to hearing apologies from others in this setting.

Kristin realized she might need to balance her passion with some softer language, given her position of relatively high power in that interaction. She could have started, for example, by praising the professor's enthusiasm for the topic and her concern for the student's learning. In future situations, Kristin decided to be more collaborative instead of trying to frame this as her being right and the other professor being wrong.

As a more-senior department member, Kristin modeled the acts of admitting mistakes and apologizing. Kristin's research finds it's more helpful when people apologize in a direct and humble way, saying, "This happened. Please forgive me," without holding their heads in shame.

As she asks in *Self-Compassion*: "What type of language do you use with yourself when you notice some flaw or make a mistake—do you insult yourself, or do you take a more kind and understanding tone?" After her mistake, she asked, "What could I have done differently?" and "What factors led to my behavior?" instead of focusing on what others might have done wrong. Practicing self-compassion includes reminding herself that "Just because my behavior wasn't good doesn't mean I'm a bad person." Our self-esteem can be unconditional instead of contingent on our behavior or performance.

REFLECT WITHOUT DWELLING ON IT OR BEATING YOURSELF UP

As Kristin says, "With self-compassion, you don't beat yourself up." Instead of saying, "I'm a bad person," consider using a constructive approach that acknowledges facts and says, "Kristin, when you used that tone of voice, she was scared. Your student was scared. You weren't very effective. It didn't help."

Reflecting on lessons learned helps you move on. Reflecting on her audiobook mistakes, Katie Anderson said, "If you keep dwelling on [your mistake], then that's counterproductive." Instead, when she encounters mistakes or setbacks, she asks herself, "How do you learn from it?" and "How do you move forward?"

Katie loves Japanese "*Daruma* dolls." She often gives these papier mâché figures to people, including myself, as gifts. A *Daruma* has two blank white eyes. When you have a goal or start a project (like Katie's audiobook or my writing of this book), you draw a black pupil on the left eye. The *Daruma* sits there as a visual reminder of your goal. When you finally achieve it, one way to celebrate is by drawing that second eye.

The base of a *Daruma* is weighted, so that when one pushes it over, it wobbles and pops back upright. It's a physical manifestation of the Japanese proverb, "Fall down seven times, get up eight."

When we fall or make a mistake, Katie reminds us, "The most important [thing is] how are you getting up and moving forward? It's not about always achieving your goal, but about how you are moving forward. And sometimes success is what you've learned rather than what you've achieved." Being kind to ourselves helps us be resilient, which means learning from our mistakes can fuel future success.

GET BETTER AT PROCESSING FAILURE AND MISTAKES

Speaker, lecturer, and publisher Dr. Cheryl Lentz is the author of *Failure Has No Alibi: Learning From the Lessons Failure Teaches.*

She notes that, when children try to walk and fall, they giggle because they don't know there's anything wrong with failing. By the time we are adults, we often learn that failure is painful, so we try to avoid it.

"We don't like that 'F' word. We don't like how it makes us feel. We don't like to fail. The point is, if you're not willing to fail, you won't succeed. Failure is a learning process. That's all it is. It's not that 'Failure is not an option.' Failure is the only option."[34]

Cheryl has come to embrace failure, saying that it has "forced me to go into different lanes." And now she goes there willingly and reinvents herself in ways that include earning her Doctor of Business Administration degree along with starting her consulting firm and podcast.

APPLY LESSONS FROM A FAILED BUSINESS TO THE NEXT

Many of my guests shared how their mistakes led to the failure of their first business, including a chiropractor, financial planner, and family therapist. Thankfully, they used those lessons to succeed in their second attempts.

Alisha Wielfaert is a leadership and resiliency coach for women and the author of *Little Failures: Learning to Build Resilience Through Everyday Setbacks, Challenges, and Obstacles.* As a runner, Alisha distinguishes between mistakes and failures, saying, "Mistakes feel more like stumbles to me, and failure feels like I'm running a race and I face-planted, and it took me a long time to get back up." A mistake doesn't feel as weighty to her.[35]

Alisha's favorite mistake was her failed yoga studio. She hoped starting a studio would help her escape corporate America. But she tried doing the studio part-time, which kept her trapped in her full-time job instead. She got burned out. Even after bringing in a business partner, the studio failed. It ended up being a learning experience that she could move on from, while the debt from the business, unfortunately, stayed with her.

After a mistake, Alisha recommends a designated grieving time, realizing some things take longer to get over. She reflects, "I am someone that likes to ruminate. And so there we'll hit this point where I'm [feeling], 'Enough, enough,' like this is no longer productive," and it becomes more self-indulgent than productive. Alisha gives herself a fixed amount of time. "If it's a little mistake, I'm going to dwell on it this weekend. And then I'm done."

She admires a friend who makes a ritual out of failures or mistakes, lighting a candle and some sage, before writing down what she is grieving over and why. "And then she does a little more self-reflection about what she gained."

Alisha also tries to reflect on what she might have gained through a mistake, writing down, and even burning the paper (working to prevent the mistake of setting her home on fire, I'm sure!). If writing it down doesn't help, Alisha suggests calling a friend or tapping into your community in different ways.

Instead of ignoring or denying mistakes, Alisha finds it healthy to call a mistake "a mistake" and a failure "a failure," even though many don't like using those words. Acknowledging the pain is important because "The pain of failure is what helps us not repeat the mistake, to change our actions, and have that foundation of learning."

It's normal to fear failure, but according to Alisha, about 5% of the population suffers from atelophobia, the chronic and persistent fear of failure. One of its symptoms is being critical of yourself or others. Alisha believes in the value of discussing mistakes or failures, as we can say:

- I was brave.

- I tried something or wanted something.

- I went after it and didn't get it right.

- It wasn't perfect—it wasn't even *close* to perfect.

- But I tried, and it set me up to do better the next time.

"Big failures don't feel good, but [you can feel good about] those ten seconds of bravery that you had to get you past the perfectionism. Even if it led to a mistake, it set you up for something greater later."

With her second business, Alisha didn't repeat the mistake of trying to do it part-time when she started her coaching business called "Yoke and Abundance." Alisha also took practical steps to avoid making a different mistake. Instead of diving head first into the new business by quitting her job, she tested the waters, conducting 25 interviews with potential clients. She was able to build out materials before leaving her job and starting the business.

"I wouldn't have done that had I not failed with that yoga studio," Alisha says.

BE INSPIRED BY THE GIRL WHO FINALLY MADE A MISTAKE

Kristin's story and reflections on self-compassion remind me of Mark Pett's delightful children's book *The Girl Who Never Made Mistakes.*

Of course, the author of a book about mistakes has a favorite mistake story to share. As a young artist, Mark inadvertently plagiarized a Pulitzer Prize award-winning editorial cartoonist's work. He learned this when he received a reply from another Pulitzer Prize recipient who "very nicely" pointed out how Mark was borrowing heavily from the cartoonists who influenced him. Mark was mortified.

Mark reflected and realized that, in his desire for greatness, he was trying to be something he was not. Mark said that letter was a real gift as it steered him toward working in his own style, using a more organic approach. Mark realizes the incident could have been a career-killer, especially if it had happened today.[36]

"I could have crawled into a hole. I could have never drawn a cartoon again. But I made a choice to view it as a gift and as an opportunity to really examine myself and what I was doing."

In Mark's book, the main character is famous throughout her school and town for never making mistakes. She takes a lot of pride in that and the paparazzi who follow her daily. The girl performs in a talent show, starting to juggle a water balloon, her pet hamster, and a salt shaker. She soon realizes her mistake—she had grabbed the pepper shaker. The hamster sneezes. The water balloon breaks. The crowd is stunned.

What does the girl do? She starts to chuckle, which turns into a laugh. The audience follows her lead and roars with laughter.

The next morning, she is not followed by fans who praise her or by paparazzi. She starts laughing about mistakes in her daily life.

As the book ends, "Now, people no longer call her 'The Girl Who Never Makes Mistakes.' They just call her 'Beatrice.'"

The book is an excellent reminder that our self-worth should come from who we are, not from what we do. Our self-worth shouldn't come from avoiding mistakes. When we remember that, we can more likely be kind and self-compassionate.

BE KIND AND CONSTRUCTIVE: ONE AND THE SAME

Leaders can do better than being nice over and over again. Putting employees in a position to repeat mistakes isn't kind at all. Replacing punishment or niceness with rigorous improvement methods means we get to the root cause of a systemic mistake in ways that prevent it from being repeated—and that might be the ultimate act of kindness.

CHAPTER FOUR

PREVENT MISTAKES

"It is in Toyota's DNA that mistakes made once will not be repeated."

—AKIO TOYODA

Chairman, Toyota Motor Corporation

M*iami Herald* columnist Greg Cote, mentioned in Chapter One, is a weekly guest host on the Dan Le Batard Show podcast (formerly an ESPN Radio program). Cote, the regular hosts, and producers are frequently fined for making small on-air mistakes—two dollars here, five dollars there, an event they celebrate by gleefully calling out, "That's a fine."

Co-host Jon "Stugotz" Weiner gets fined for reading the internet wrong or clearing his throat into the microphone. Le Batard is punished for getting a name wrong (or mixing up two people), saying somebody is dead (when they're not), or speaking in a tone that sounds too strident (which he often does).

Yet, they make mistakes all the time. Le Batard complained in a 2018 episode, "Do you realize how much I talk on this microphone? And how many mistakes do I make?" Executive Producer Mike Ryan said, "This is about limiting those mistakes because you're afraid of the fine."

Le Batard yelled (probably getting fined for his tone), "You're not limiting mistakes, and I'm not making any fewer mistakes. I'm only making more mistakes, and the coffers get filled." The show does celebrate mistakes in a way, since their annual show-awards event has included categories for "Best Mistake" and "Worst Dan Mistake," like the time he referred to the band Blink-182 as "Blink-192." Dan protested, "Do I get fined for that? I thought it was just people's names!"

You can't punish your way to perfection—on the radio, on a podcast, or in any workplace.

The system of fines continues to this day, and I think they realize that it doesn't prevent mistakes. But with very small fines and a little bit of fun, the show doesn't seem like a culture of fear. As Le Batard often says, they embrace mistakes. The system is effective in what might be its actual intent—to create laughs and fill ten hours of show time weekly.

REPLACE FEAR WITH MISTAKE-PROOFING

Fear and punishment drive people to get better at hiding mistakes when they could channel that energy into preventing them. When they can't be hidden, repeated mistakes illustrate how punishment accomplishes nothing beyond deflecting blame from leaders.

One of my heroes, W. Edwards Deming, who also deeply influenced Toyota executives, shared what may be the most important recommendation in his famed "14 Points for Management": "Drive out fear, so that everyone may work effectively for the company."[37]

Driving out fear means, in part, that everyone can feel safe to speak up about mistakes and improvement ideas, as discussed in Chapters Five and Six. Leaders can also alleviate the fear of making mistakes, to begin with, when they combine the right methods and mindsets.

Starting with mindset, as former Toyota leader Darril Wilburn says, "It's a leader's responsibility to create a system in which people can be successful." Therefore, it's the leader's responsibility to drive out fear. This includes creating work systems where it's easier to do the right thing and more difficult to make a mistake. This responsibility doesn't fall solely on the shoulders of leaders. They also engage their team members in designing effective mistake-proofing methods.

Mistake-proofing, or *"poka yoke"* in Japanese, is a core method within the Toyota Production System. It's a mindset based on the idea that people want to do good work, but they're imperfect. So, leaders have an obligation to help.

You might not think of Toyota as an entrepreneurial company today, but it started small, in 1926, as a manufacturer of weaving looms based on patents held by founder Sakichi Toyoda. One of his key innovations was a mechanism that would automatically stop a loom when a thread broke, preventing it from cranking out more defective cloth. This innovation also led to huge productivity increases. One worker could now oversee upward of

30 to 50 machines, walking over to respond to problems when they were detected, instead of having to continually hover over a single machine.

It's said Toyota originally used the phrase *"baka yoke,"* which means "idiot-proofing." Many decades ago, that term upset a Japanese factory worker who, correctly, complained that they weren't an idiot. We should also avoid saying "fool-proofing" or "dummy-proofing," regardless of how often we hear them spoken around us.

Professor John Grout, the former dean of the Campbell School of Business at Berry College, is an expert on mistakes, receiving some of his early education in the field from Toyota leaders. He thinks mistake-proofing should be called "slip-proofing," as it's easier to prevent execution errors than bad decisions (planning mistakes). One common slip is closing a file without saving it. The "Are you sure?" dialogue box tries to protect us, but as John points out, we're likely to just click "Yes" out of habit. That's a slip on top of a slip—and one that's hard to prevent. Using software that continually autosaves your work completely eliminates that risk (to my benefit, as I write this book in Google Docs).

IS THE SOFTWARE MISTAKE-PRONE OR MISTAKE-PROOF?

Software developers often incorporate mistake-proofing into the software or websites that we use. For example, when we create a new password for a website, we are usually prompted to type the password twice. This protects us from setting our password incorrectly due to a single typo. Some websites prevent you from copying and pasting that first password to protect you from pasting a password that includes a typo. Of course, typing the password twice still leaves open the possibility that you repeat the same typo. The impact of any of these mistakes is usually mitigated by the ability to reset your password.

On the other hand, the design of software can invite, if not guarantee, mistakes. In a recent meeting held on Microsoft Teams, my colleague Sara said she was about to share a document, but she disappeared. Returning a few seconds later, Sara admitted she accidentally clicked the "Leave" button. We all laughed it off instead of being unkind to her. We moved on with the meeting.

I wouldn't blame her (or others) for clicking the wrong button. The "Leave" button is large and red, and her "eyes just got drawn to it," Sara said. The "Share" button is slightly to the left of "Leave," without much of a gap between them.

Some might blame Sara for "user error" and leave it at that. "The users should be more careful," they might say, but that's not effective. Sara was certainly not the only human to mis-click "Leave" that day. There would be fewer incorrect clicks if Microsoft increased the distance between "Share" and "Leave." On my laptop screen, there is plenty of space to move all the other buttons further left (in the March 2023 version). A larger gap might not prevent 100% of those mistakes, but it would help. I'd take progress over perfection.

In comparison, the Zoom "Share Screen" is a large green button in the center of the toolbar. "End" is a large red button located on the far right, next to "More," which is likely clicked far less often than "Share." This layout reduces the risk of a user mistakenly clicking "End." Better design means fewer mistakes, and that's true for software *and* our work processes.

THE MISTAKES THAT MAKE US

One time, serving as host for the weekly KaiNexus Zoom meeting, I needed to leave early. Sure enough, I clicked "End," which appears in the lower right, where "Leave" also appears for attendees. When the host clicks "End," Zoom presents two buttons: "End Meeting for All" on top and in bright red, with "Leave Meeting" as a dark button on the bottom.

That time, my eyes (and cursor) were magically drawn to the big, bold, red "End Meeting for All" option. It was my mistake. That slip was slightly embarrassing, and it took a while to get everybody to rejoin the meeting so I could apologize before leaving correctly this time.

Having made the mistake once made me pretty mindful about not repeating it. But that wears off quickly, another reason why reminders or "Be careful" admonitions aren't effective. KaiNexus learned from my mistake and changed the host role to a colleague who would likely never need to leave early. I'm likely to make that mistake again, as will others. Have you?

DISTINGUISH BETWEEN PLANNING
AND EXECUTION MISTAKES

The one time my wife tried making a soufflé (to surprise me for my birthday, which was really sweet of her), she mistakenly used tartar sauce instead of cream of tartar. This was a planning mistake—based on a lack of knowledge. She didn't know that the creamy squeeze-bottle sauce differed from the glass-jarred powdered spice that's confusingly called a "cream." You might ask, "How didn't she know that?" Don't blame her, as she is allergic to fish, so she never eats tartar sauce.

That soufflé didn't pan out. This was 2001, when we didn't have Google constantly at the ready for us to double-check such things. She made an assumption and learned pretty quickly it was a mistake when the soufflé didn't rise, and we began to investigate. I double-checked if she was OK with me using the story, so I'm not making a mistake by sharing it.

Now, if I use cayenne pepper instead of cinnamon in a recipe, that's likely an execution mistake (and I'm dooming myself to this someday). Grabbing the wrong spice from the pantry is certainly something I've done before, even if it wasn't as easily detectable as adding cayenne pepper to, say, a cinnamon roll. *Achoo!*

In that last paragraph, I originally typed "cinnamon role," an execution mistake that I caught and fixed immediately. I've seen others make that mistake online, and it's impossible to know if it was a planning mistake (they didn't know the correct word) or if it was an execution mistake (a typo, like mine).

PREVENT OR QUICKLY FIX EXECUTION MISTAKES

As noted above, execution mistakes can be further broken down into "slips" and "lapses"—physical and mental mistakes. For example, I know how to spell the word "mistake." I usually type it correctly, which I did in this paragraph three times so far. I double-checked my count, as I could have made a mistake. Now it's four.

Quite often, and ironically, my fingers move in a sequence that types out "mistkae." And I'm generally a speedy and accurate touch typist. Thankfully, tools like Spellcheck and Autocorrect usually detect such mistakes, but Spellcheck wouldn't catch "cinnamon role," while a fancy grammar-checking tool probably would.

Apple iOS's "Auto-Correction" feature, ironically, makes its own mistakes. It once turned my text message to Greg Jacobson, MD, CEO of KaiNexus, from my intended "will send webex" into "will send weed." That's one we still laugh about.

Another embarrassing slip, a mental mistake, was when I forgot to click "Record" when starting an episode of my *Lean Blog Interviews* podcast. I owned up to the mistake instead of blaming a technical glitch. The guest kindly replied, "That's OK—we'll call that first time a practice session. We'll do it again." I was already upset with myself. If that guest had yelled at me for wasting their time, it wouldn't have made me less likely to repeat that mistake.

As a systemic fix, Zoom, which I currently use to record podcasts, can be set to start recording automatically when the meeting starts. Using that feature solves one problem but might create another. A recording that starts automatically captures any initial sound check and casual conversation, and I might forget to edit the first part out of the recording. The impact of publishing those moments could be mildly embarrassing or catastrophic, depending on what was said!

Partway through the pandemic, Zoom added a large pop-up window that asks each participant to click and give explicit permission to be recorded. Once people get used to clicking on that recording notification, it's more likely that a guest might ask, "Hey, is this not recording?" if I started welcoming them to the episode without clicking "Record." I was saved by somebody speaking up recently, at the start of a KaiNexus webinar, as described in Chapter Six.

USE CHECKLISTS TO PREVENT EXECUTION MISTAKES

At KaiNexus, I helped the co-founders bring the software to market in 2011 and have helped the founders cultivate a culture of continuous improvement. This is possible in a company with a high degree of psychological safety (as measured by the company through an anonymous survey) and an intent to deal with mistakes constructively. As CEO Greg Jacobson, MD, told me, "You can't have a culture of continuous improvement without learning from mistakes."

I can't recall anyone ever getting upset with me for a mistake, and I'm thankful for that. The leaders and the team always focus on understanding what happened, what we can learn, and what we'll do differently going forward. This strengthens the feeling of psychological safety, which helps us more effectively prevent future mistakes.

Organizing and hosting (or presenting) a monthly webinar for seven years has created many opportunities for me to make (and prevent) mistakes. Greg (an emergency-medicine physician by training) and I were the most frequent presenters in the early years of the webinar series. Many healthcare organizations have adopted checklists from the aviation industry, which inspired us to create a webinar checklist.

We anticipated and listed things that could go wrong (due to a mistake or outside factors) to form the basis of the checklist. We later broke this out into two separate checklists—one that covers everything that should happen during the planning phases prior to the day of the webinar and another that covers the webinar itself and our final fifteen minutes of prep before going live.

For example, the table below shows some items that appeared in the original checklist. The checklist grew and evolved as we made new mistakes (and as we identified new risks proactively).

Possible Problem or Mistake	Checklist Countermeasure
iPhone or iPad makes noise	Put devices into vibrate mode
Moving mouse to lower right corner of screen makes slides disappear and desktop appear	Turn off "hot corners" on the Mac
Having wrong information about the upcoming webinar	Confirm this when reviewing slides before uploading for attendees

Using the word "countermeasure" instead of "solution" in the checklist is intentional and, I think, meaningful. The word "solution" seems very absolute and definitive, as in "this will completely solve the problem." The word "countermeasure" suggests making a situation better while leaving open the possibility that a countermeasure might have side effects, including the creation of a new problem.

Of course, I also use a checklist to prevent the repeat of mistakes that I've made producing *My Favorite Mistake*. Mistakes that led to checklist items have included me not notifying a guest that their episode had been released and not getting the transcript created before the episode's release.

PRIORITIZING THE PROBLEMS OR
MISTAKES WE NEED TO PREVENT

When facing a multitude of problems or mistakes that would lead to varying degrees of damage, we might need to prioritize our efforts. A helpful method created by the U.S. military in the late 1940s is "Failure Mode and Effects Analysis," or FMEA. The tool helps us list the ways our product or service could fail or break ("failure modes") in ways that have negative effects on customers.

The first step in the FMEA protocol is having a cross-functional team list mistakes or failures that are known to occur or be possible. For each failure mode, the team discusses and documents how the customer is impacted.

The second step is evaluating and scoring (on a scale of 1 to 10) each failure mode on three different factors, ideally using data (or, if need be, our best educated guesses):

- Severity (10 being most severe impact)

- Occurrence (10 being most likely to occur)

- Detection (10 being most difficult to detect when it occurs)

The three numbers are multiplied together for each failure mode to create a score, called the Risk Priority Number (RPN), which allows us to sort and prioritize our failure-mode-prevention efforts, generally working to prevent items with the highest scores first if we don't have the time or resources to address them all. With our webinar checklist, the cost of our preventive measures is low, so we could implement them all without prioritizing.

If we are taking a road trip, we could do a small FMEA exercise to consider possible risks or mistakes, along with preventive measures, with a partial list of possible failure modes shown in the table as a hypothetical exercise.

Failure Mode	Severity	Likelihood	Detection	Score
Tire blows out	8	3	7	168
Wheel falls off while driving	10	2	5	100
Difficult to see through windshield	3	6	3	48
Running out of fuel	6	2	1	12

Assigning scores is quite often a judgment call. Running out of gas (or battery charge) in the middle of a desert on a 120° F degree day could be a severity of 10, while doing so in or near a major city might be a 3. A wheel falling off at high speed can be prevented by checking the tightness of our lug nuts before a trip. We can take other actions, including replacing wiper blades, ensuring our washer fluid is filled, checking the depth of our tire treads, and being mindful of mapping out refueling stops before we depart. Even if the exact scores are not fully agreed upon by those involved, the exercise of discussing risks and preventive measures can be quite helpful.

Prevent Mistakes

LEARN FROM MISTAKES TO PREVENT REPEATS

In our original webinar checklist, we identified some problems that could arise immediately before starting the presentation, such as a microphone problem or slow Wi-Fi, each of which might take a few minutes to resolve. As a result, we ask presenters to join webinars fifteen minutes early so we can complete our final webinar-prep checklist. We don't usually need the entire time, but the extra buffer allows us to troubleshoot and rectify any problems while minimizing stress and the risk of starting late.

One time, our presenter thought the webinar started an hour later than scheduled, at 1 p.m. Central time instead of Eastern. When the presenter didn't arrive fifteen minutes early for the final prep, I called, and he was able to join the webinar in time. Crisis averted. Thankfully, he wasn't out to lunch. If the standard had been to join five minutes early, we would have started late, providing an opportunity to learn and increase that buffer.

We followed our KaiNexus habit of looking at how our process caused the problem and not blaming that individual for being wrong. We found that our webinar system at the time didn't send an electronic calendar invitation to presenters. This meant I had to manually email the day and time to them, which left open the possibility of miscommunication. Owning that mistake, I adjusted by sending formal calendar invitations that would adjust for time zones, still facing the risk that the presenter might fail to add the invite to their calendar. This countermeasure has since become obsolete, since the Zoom Webinars platform sends a formal calendar invitation to the participants when we add them as a panelist.

Here are some additional examples from our checklist:

Mistake/Problem	Added to Checklist:
Forgot to get the presenter bio for making a proper introduction	Get the speaker bio in advance
Post-webinar follow-up email had a link to the wrong recording page	Ensure the follow-up email was set up correctly, and do so further in advance
Presenter didn't understand what the KaiNexus software platform did and talked about possibly starting a company to do what we do	Ensure the presenter has a high-level understanding of the KaiNexus software platform
Browser tab makes noise	Ensure that social media sites or other tabs that give alerts are closed
Echo came through the webinar platform	Ensure everybody is wearing headphones
Sound was bad because the wrong microphone was being used	Add a microphone-source-confir-mation step to the checklist

As part of our checklist pruning, we recognized that our current system, Zoom, had better echo-prevention technology, so we no longer need to insist that everybody wear headphones. That said, part of our checklist includes doing a private sound check, so if we did detect an echo for some reason, putting on headphones is usually an easy countermeasure before we formally begin.

We do our best, but we're not perfect. We make mistakes. We try to learn and prevent them, but you never really know if a countermeasure is effective until you test it. We might make mistakes in our mistake-proofing efforts, but that provides additional opportunities to choose learning and improvement over punishment, as discussed in Chapter Six.

CHECKLISTS HELP ONLY WHEN YOU USE THEM

Atul Gawande, MD's, book *The Checklist Manifesto* describes the power of checklists in various industries. Gawande emphasizes that checklists help prevent even the best surgeons, with flawless track records, from making a catastrophic mistake when they might be tired or distracted. Checklists can help any of us in the same way.

John Grout warns that checklists are a relatively weak form of mistake-proofing, but warning signs or admonitions to be careful are even less effective.[38] Even a perfectly designed checklist is completely ineffective when unused, a lesson I've learned the hard way.

After successfully producing a few webinars without any problems or mistakes, I've fallen into the temptation of thinking, *I've got this; I don't need this checklist anymore.* Oops. Not using the checklist has led to mistakes, such as not sharing a PDF of the slides with attendees. I've learned from that meta-mistake and use the checklist diligently every time.

While we try to be proactive, we often make new mistakes that we didn't anticipate. Almost every time we hold a KaiNexus webinar, I discover a new possibility for mistakes, either a new opportunity that has popped up because the technology has changed or something I hadn't noticed before.

Our checklists have grown to about 100 items, with roughly half of them added in reaction to a mistake that was made.

We occasionally review the checklist, pruning items that are now unnecessary, so that we can save time in its ongoing use. Effectively preventing (and learning from) mistakes isn't just about the checklist. It's also a matter of culture.

THE NEED FOR MISTAKE-PROOFING IN HEALTHCARE

Mistakes in healthcare, such as giving the wrong medication or mixing up laboratory specimens, can lead to serious harm or death. Far too often, healthcare workplaces lack mistake-proofing mindsets, relying far too heavily on admonitions to be careful. Hospital computer systems often present "Are you sure?" warnings when the severity of a mistake is far worse than failing to save a file. Research shows that the effectiveness of these alerts is "modest at best," and "alert fatigue" develops, where clinicians reflexively click through and ignore alerts.[39]

With imperfect mistake-proofing, it's far too common for a patient to be the victim of harm, with the involved caregivers being what some call the "second victims." These healthcare providers are traumatized by feelings including shame, guilt, anxiety, grief, and depression, even when they are not explicitly blamed or punished by leaders. This reaction often drives people to leave healthcare altogether. Mistakes cannot be totally eliminated, which is why we can provide support that helps people learn how to be more resilient. And, it's better to also focus on systems that prevent mistakes and harm.

One example of mistake-proofing in healthcare is the use of bar codes, where a nurse scans a patient's wristband and the medication at the bedside to confirm a match. But when bar-code-scanning systems are slow or unreliable, nurses who are overburdened often feel pressured to create workarounds that save time but increase the risk of a mistake. For example, nurses might print additional copies of patient wristbands, allowing them to batch up the scanning of multiple meds and wristbands at the medication cabinet.

In response to the workaround, the hospital might make it more difficult to print duplicate wristbands, when a better solution would be making the bar-code system faster and more reliable. When employees circumvent mistake-proofing devices, leaders should ask "Why?" instead of blaming and punishing them. Inquiring with language such as, "Help me understand how that happened" or "What got in the way of normal practice?" can seem less blaming, which better involves the caregiver in the problem-solving process.

Surgical mistakes are more likely to be prevented when the checklist also includes a step where the entire team performs a "time-out" that includes everybody introducing themselves by name and role. That, with the addition of wearing surgical caps displaying each person's name and role, enables better communication and increased levels of mutual respect. Breaking down the traditional surgical hierarchies and inviting input can help people feel safer speaking up.

When pre-surgical checklists are poorly designed, they take too long, and surgeons might be tempted to skip them—a planning mistake that could lead to an execution mistake, like a wrong-side surgery. Again, if surgeons circumvent the mistake-proofing, leaders should ask why surgeons might feel pressured to save time. Why have they fallen behind schedule, and why do they need to catch up?

A hospital can reduce delays by addressing the root causes of problems that cause schedules to slip. This might include ensuring that no surgical instruments are missing or dirty when a procedure is about to start. Or, we can mistake-proof the mistake-proofing, by not allowing the surgeon to have a scalpel for the initial incision until the checklist and time-out have been followed.

"The way to know you have a good checklist is if it speeds you up," says John Grout, using the example of a checklist he uses to pack before a trip. After years of using and refining this checklist, he has a lot of faith in it. He'll ask if there's anything unusual he doesn't normally bring, and that item will get written down on this checklist. "The longer the checklist, the more doomed to death it is," he adds.

He says that designing mistake-proofing devices takes a lot of thought and that you need to test their effectiveness in actual use. We could ask if the actual outcomes of the mistake-proofing match our expected outcomes (zero mistakes). If not, we need to detect this, learn, and adjust.

USE SMALL MISTAKES TO PREVENT LARGE ONES

Greg Jacobson, MD, the co-founder and CEO of KaiNexus, has worked as an emergency-medicine physician in dozens of hospital environments where leaders shamed people for mistakes. He decries how they miss out on opportunities to learn from minor mistakes that go unreported.

For example, giving a patient 600 mg of a pain reliever instead of 800 mg might lead to mild discomfort instead of harm. The lack of harm doesn't mean the hospital should ignore the incident. It is a warning sign about general problems with the medication-administration process. Bad processes, not bad people, cause most problems, as Greg agrees.[40]

When people choose not to report these small problems, they fail to address the underlying causes. Nobody asks questions such as: What led to the dosing mistake? Was there a miscommunication? Was the wrong medicine loaded into one of the automated medication-cabinet drawers? What needs to happen so this mistake doesn't happen for the next patient or the next caregiver?

Greg wants organizations to "celebrate" mistakes. That doesn't mean they're happy when a patient gets a lower dose of pain reliever. It means celebrating the "opportunity to look at the process to see if we could make it safer." Otherwise, the next medication error could be a patient receiving ten times the ordered amount of the blood-thinner heparin, which could be a life-threatening mistake.

PREVENTING MISTAKES OR MITIGATING THEIR IMPACT

While this will quickly become an outdated scenario, think about the range of mistake-proofing techniques we encounter at a gas station. Some mistakes are almost completely prevented. For example, the gas station generally forces customers to pay before pumping gas, preventing a customer from forgetting to pay (or intentionally stealing fuel).

We could make many mistakes in choosing the wrong fuel for our vehicles. Some mistakes are prevented, and some are less likely, due to certain design choices. One example of a small and relatively harmless slip is pushing the wrong button on the pump, selecting the wrong octane or grade of unleaded gas.

If you have a vehicle that runs well on lower-octane fuel, pressing the mid-grade or high-octane button is a little costly, but harmless. If your vehicle requires or recommends high-octane fuel, selecting a lower-grade fuel means your engine won't perform as well, but you'll still reach your destination.

Putting diesel (or other alternative fuels, like ethanol-based E85) into a gasoline engine can cause damage requiring costly repairs. It helps that those fuels come from nozzles (or pumps) that are separate from the one that dispenses multiple grades of unleaded gasoline. Having handles with different colors reduces, but doesn't eliminate, the risk of using the wrong fuel. A sticker or a yellow fuel cap might attempt to remind people of the risk, but warning signs are a very weak form of mistake-proofing.

Thankfully for drivers of gasoline-fueled vehicles, the dispensing nozzle for diesel fuel is larger, so that it doesn't fit into the gas tank. Since the gas nozzle fits into the larger diesel gas tank opening, it's not mistake-proofed in the other direction, leaving open the possibility of a costly and damaging mistake that will quickly disable a diesel engine.

You might ask why the nozzles aren't designed to prevent the more-damaging mistake of putting gasoline in a diesel engine? When unleaded gasoline was introduced, its nozzle was made smaller to prevent drivers of those vehicles from filling up with leaded gasoline. As a result, we're left today with having to be careful about not putting gas into a diesel engine.

If your company has a fleet of vehicles using a mix of fuel types, it's only a matter of time before somebody puts gas into a diesel engine. They might not be aware that they did it. In the FMEA method, the detectability might be low, while the severity is high. If the driver does realize they mistakenly filled the diesel engine with gas, trying to drive will only make it worse. It's time to call a tow truck!

The warning signs around a gas pump illustrate things that are not (or cannot be) mistake-proofed. We are warned not to smoke around the pumps. I don't know how you would mistake-proof that, other than banning smoking. A small sign reminds us to shut off our engine before fueling. This *could* be mistake-proofed, but at an expense to vehicle owners, if regulators required fuel doors that remained locked unless the vehicle was turned off.

In your workplace, look for warning signs with phrases like "Be careful," "Please remember," or "Don't forget." These signs illustrate opportunities to use more effective mistake-proofing methods. If signs worked, we'd be able to eliminate surgical errors by putting large signs in every operating room that read, "Don't operate on the wrong side, wrong site, or wrong patient."

If we can't perfectly prevent mistakes, John Grout says one way we prevent problems is by asking, "How can I make this process fail in a way that's benign instead of in a way that's terrible?"

If you make the mistake of driving off without returning the fuel nozzle to the pump, you won't be the first. I hope I never make this mistake. I've never seen a warning sign reading, "Don't forget to return the nozzle." That would be ineffective, but it's also unnecessary.

If you try driving off without returning the nozzle, it's usually designed to fail benignly. A quick-release connector will break off, cutting off the gas flow and preventing spills and the risk of fire or explosion. The pump was designed with the expectation that people will occasionally make that mistake. We know we need to put the nozzle back, but the many distractions of modern life could lead somebody to forget—a "lapse."

The benign-but-embarrassing failure might cause minor damage to the connector if one keeps driving and dragging it along. Hopefully, a driver would hear an unusual noise as they drive off, prompting them to stop, thereby reducing the damage. Another form of mistake-proofing, by the way, is the need to press the brake or clutch pedal before shifting into drive. This prevents us from unexpectedly speeding off because we mistakenly put our foot on the accelerator.

In a more modern example, we don't see EVs rolling down the road dragging charging cables behind. That is mistake-proofed by a pin in the charging connector that tells the vehicle if the cable is connected, even if only part-way. The vehicle will not shift out of "Park" if it's still plugged in.

Even with creative and diligent mistake-proofing efforts, mistakes will still occur. That's why leaders need to create conditions for everybody to feel safe enough to speak up, as discussed next in Chapter Five.

Since entrepreneurs or managers cannot prevent all mistakes, how can we design systems where failures are benign instead of terrible? It's really difficult to mistake-proof bad decisions. Thankfully, one way to mitigate our risk is by utilizing small tests of change, using small mistakes to prevent bigger ones that can harm our business, as we'll learn more about in Chapter Seven.

HELP EVERYONE TO SPEAK UP

*"For knowledge work to flourish,
the workplace must be one where people feel able to
share their knowledge! This means sharing concerns,
questions, mistakes, and half-formed ideas."*

—Amy Edmondson, PhD

The Fearless Organization

"Hey, everyone, I made a mistake this week."
In a KaiNexus company meeting, a customer-success manager, Kaleigh, explained how she had been waiting for a reply email from a customer. Or so she thought until she learned her outgoing message was actually stuck in her "Draft" folder. Nobody mocked or criticized her. I've made that email mistake. So has CEO Greg Jacobson, MD, who admitted so in response. Greg's reaction was kind and constructive, providing some consolation and sharing the steps he takes to prevent that mistake, or to make sure messages aren't stuck there very long.

That simple exchange illustrates a culture of psychological safety, with transparency being the sunlight needed to cultivate our ability to learn from the mistakes of others. A few minutes later, Greg told a quick story about something else that went wrong, punctuating it with, "It's great we made that mistake," because he (and the employee he was working with) learned from it.

When an employee chooses to speak up, it isn't a matter of courage or character; it's a function of culture. If employees aren't speaking up, we must ask, "Why?" People won't feel safe speaking up if they fear being ridiculed, marginalized, or punished. Leaders can cultivate an environment where people feel safer, if not absolutely safe, to admit mistakes.

And that doesn't mean creating an optimistically named program like "Speak Up for Safety," as I've seen General Motors and some health systems do. These programs assume employees don't want to speak up, offering encouragement or admonitions. But employees *do* want to speak up, especially on important matters like employee and patient safety.

Asking people to speak up is a great start, but leaders must reward employees for doing so. I don't mean financial rewards. It often starts with simply saying, "Thank you" when they admit or point out a mistake.

Research by Ethan Burris, PhD, Senior Associate Dean for Academic Affairs at the McCombs School of Business at the University of Texas at Austin, discovered two primary reasons why employees don't use their voice in the workplace: fear and futility.[41] In a culture of fear and punishment, employees will understandably protect themselves by staying quiet, at a great cost to the organization.

Medical professionals generally want to report mistakes as a way to spur improvement but face a myriad of technical and cultural barriers—including fear and futility. If they're no longer afraid of being punished for reporting the mistake, doing so is often extremely time-consuming. The 30 minutes spent entering details into a website is time they can't afford to take away from ongoing patient care in busy, often-under-staffed departments.

Eliminating fear is crucial, but we can't replace it with futility, where people shift from saying, "I'm afraid to speak up" to "I would speak up, but it's not worth the effort." If pointing out mistakes doesn't lead to improvement and the prevention of repeats, people get discouraged and stop using their voice for good.

Leaders must address both the fear factor and the futility factor. When it's safer and easier to report mistakes, and when doing so leads to action and improvement, people are more likely to continue filing reports. It's also kind and helpful to thank people every time they report a mistake, no matter how small.

WHEN A SURGEON ISN'T SAFE TO ADMIT A MISTAKE

Companies like Toyota create an environment that reduces the number of likely mistakes while helping employees feel safe speaking up when they make a mistake or see one. Let's compare that to a story told by anesthesiologist David Mayer, MD. As a resident, in 1985, David was assigned to provide anesthesia care for a patient's right-sided inguinal-hernia-repair procedure.[42]

Before the start of the procedure, the attending surgeon (the experienced teacher) was delayed by the need to answer a question outside the room. The resident surgeon (the student) made an incision on the *patient's left side*.

Two minutes later, the attending walked in, looked, and said, "I thought this was a right-sided inguinal hernia." That's right—the incision had been made on the incorrect side. Not right but wrong. Not right but left.

"Everybody was horrified," David recalls, including the shaken surgical resident who dropped to one knee and had to be helped to a chair in the corner of the room to gather herself. The surgical attending calmly closed the unnecessary incision and performed the correct procedure on the correct side. Because of the need to cover the unnecessary incision, "There would be no hiding the mistake" physically, as David recalled.

Later, the patient smiled at David in the recovery room and exclaimed, "Today's my lucky day! The surgeon discovered I had two hernias and fixed them both! I'll only miss one day of work, not two!"

David was "dumbfounded" to learn that the attending surgeon had lied to the patient about a second hernia instead of disclosing the mistake. After what felt like an eternity, David replied, "Yes, it is your lucky day." As a resident, David feared it would be a career-ending move if he contradicted the surgeon and spoke up about the mistake.

"The shame-and-blame culture of our medical profession guaranteed that it would be only a matter of time before our team suffered the consequences of our error. I was terrified this medical error would damage my professional career, and I wondered if I would be disciplined by the hospital, suspended by my department, or face criminal charges," instead of being able to focus on the patient.[43]

Had this mistake been revealed, David says, any investigation would have focused on assigning blame. "Every resident physician was conditioned early in training that someone is at fault when things go wrong," he says, instead of looking for problems with processes and systems.

Thankfully, recent medical education teaches modern concepts about mistakes and improvement more often. Greg Jacobson, MD, who completed his emergency-medicine residency in 2004, was taught an estimate that says "85% of defects or errors are caused by an inadequate process." The number could be even higher, but the point is to stop assuming that 85% of defects are caused by the so-called "bad apples" in the workplace. Even with some progress being made in some organizations, "naming, blaming, and shaming" is still the norm in healthcare today.

Performing the incision on the wrong side illustrates the concept of a systemic error, since many people were involved. We don't know the root cause in this case, but we would want to ask constructive questions in the immediate aftermath for the purposes of learning and process improvement. How could this occur? What allowed it to happen? How far upstream did any miscommunication begin? Did somebody drape the wrong side of the patient? If so, why?

Perhaps the resident erred by not waiting for the attending to arrive before starting. Or the attending had previously yelled at (or more subtly punished) the resident for waiting to start cases, which might have led her to go ahead and start. Or the surgery schedule had fallen behind, and there was pressure to keep things moving. I can only speculate here, and doing so would be a mistake during a real problem-solving situation.

FOLLOWING A SLIP WITH A BAD DECISION

The attending surgeon was the highest-ranking person in the room. He was involved in the initial mistake. The resident surgeon made the wrong incision, but the attending surgeon's job is to supervise and teach. Surgical time-outs and checklists weren't yet being used in 1985.

David knew the attending surgeon had made a bad decision by lying to the patient about finding the second hernia. It may be surprising, but healthcare has learned that patients are less likely to file a lawsuit after a mistake if the surgeon admits it and apologizes. We're all human. We all make mistakes. We all appreciate honesty, empathy, and an apology.

The attending surgeon had consciously decided to cover up the wrong-side mistake. The wrong-side incision was a systemic failure. The cultural elements involved in hiding the mistake are even more systemic. If the attending surgeon feared punishment, I can understand why he didn't speak up. It illustrates why leaders need to remove barriers to honest disclosures, including taking steps that create the conditions for higher levels of psychological safety.

WHEN "NEVER EVENTS" HAPPEN . . . ALL THE TIME

Many healthcare professionals still don't feel safe speaking up about mistakes. One study estimates that about 40 wrong-site or wrong-side surgeries occur each week across the U.S., but according to The Joint Commission, only 68 wrong-site surgeries were reported in 2020. Healthcare experts agree that incidents and harm of all types are underreported by a large margin, but by how much? One estimate suggests only 3 to 5% of errors are reported.[44] That indicates it's still not safe to speak up. Or they feel like it's futile. Or both.

Healthcare has optimistically started referring to mistakes like these as "never events." They should never happen; they are completely preventable. The oft-prescribed solution to wrong-side, wrong-site, or wrong-patient surgeries is the checklist, as introduced in Chapter Four. To prevent mistakes, surgical teams should always take steps that create a positive confirmation that they have the correct patient on the table for the correct procedure. The surgeon marks or signs near the surgical site with the patient's confirmation while they are still awake.

A combination of these practices, including a time-out, is often referred to, also optimistically, as the "universal protocol," meaning it should be done everywhere, every single time. If the protocol were truly universal, we'd be closer to the goal of never making these mistakes.

Again, it's more about the culture than the checklist. At a Wisconsin health system, former CEO Dr. John Toussaint recalls one of their hospitals had four wrong-site surgeries over an eight-week period in 2004. Problems "slipped under the radar" of senior leaders because "everybody simply kept quiet."[45] Eventually, through the medical peer-review process, then-president Kathryn Correia was informed of the mistakes. She immediately shut down the surgical suites, meaning no more procedures until they had a plan to "ensure the safety of every patient." The surgeons agreed to have an independent auditor present at every surgery to lead the timeout, to ensure the universal protocol was followed.

As Toussaint wrote, "There was no upside to reporting errors in our shame-and-blame culture, so most opportunities for learning and improvement were lost." Correia realized that she needed to improve the culture-change efforts.

Today, hospitals make mistakes related to surgical procedures:

- Not doing the time-out or checklist (or just going through the motions to check the box)

- Assuming the time-out or checklist isn't needed because it was skipped a few times and didn't lead immediately to patient harm

- Not speaking up about a surgeon skipping the timeout or checklist (because they didn't feel safe)

- An executive *not* shutting down operating rooms to investigate after becoming aware of mistakes, whether they lead to harm or not

Getting to "never" also requires a culture that helps anybody in the operating room feel safe to speak up to raise a concern, even if that delays or stops the work. Toyota has this culture, in circumstances where the stakes are generally much lower. Some health systems perform better in getting closer to "never events" actually never happening, not because of luck or the surgeon's skill, but because of better systems and cultures of higher psychological safety.

Help Everyone to Speak Up

THE ANESTHESIOLOGIST'S MISTAKE SPARKED
HIS PATIENT-SAFETY CAREER

So why did David refer to this incident as his favorite mistake when he wasn't the one who made the incision or lied to the patient? David says his mistakes were, first, not challenging the attending surgeon and, second, not telling the truth to the patient, even though being open and honest "was the right thing to do." But again, speaking up is not a matter of character—it's the result of culture.

David says that during his seven years of formal medical-school education, "Nobody ever talked about what happens when we make an error or harm a patient. I also never had a discussion about what we do and how we respond when an error occurs."

David describes the behaviors he saw that day as "deny and defend, lie about it, get away with it." Doing this keeps people out of trouble, but it doesn't lead to improvement. "When we hide errors like that—when we bury them within our own little silos—we don't learn. The mistake that I've lived with for 35 years has shaped my career in many ways."

David learned how hierarchical and punitive workplace cultures prevent people from feeling safe. Residents might not feel safe challenging an attending, and nurses or operating-room techs might not feel safe challenging the physicians. It's understandable when people don't speak up if doing so creates the risk of loss or harm on personal or professional levels.

The wrong-side surgery incident sparked David's passion for improving patient safety, not just for his anesthesia patients but also more broadly. Beyond his direct patient-care work, David has served as the executive director for the MedStar Institute for Quality and Safety at the Maryland-based MedStar health system and as CEO of the nonprofit Patient Safety Movement Foundation.

David has worked tirelessly to improve systems and cultures so others would feel safer, which makes it safer for patients, as they benefit from improvements that occur when learning is the focus instead of naming, blaming, and shaming. This also relieves providers from carrying the burden of lying about and hiding their mistakes.

MODEL AND REWARD THE RIGHT BEHAVIORS

A culture of learning from mistakes requires that each person feels a reasonably high level of psychological safety. Timothy R. Clark, PhD, succinctly defines psychological safety as "a culture of rewarded vulnerability."[46]

A "vulnerable act" exposes us to the risk of harm or loss, personally or professionally. We're describing an action, not the person. Basically, any interaction between two or more human beings can be vulnerable, some more than others. A specific *act* might be vulnerable to some degree for a specific situation. Unlike physical safety, where we might say a particular act is inherently risky for all (such as working up high without a safety harness), the perceived level of risk for acts, such as pointing out a mistake, is situational and individual.

The level of psychological safety that we feel will vary from person to person. You might feel safe in one team, while a colleague feels relatively unsafe in that same setting. Our feeling of safety could vary due to our differing interactions with leaders and members of that team. We each might be influenced differently by memories of bad experiences in previous workplaces, where speaking up and admitting a mistake led to being punished or fired. It's a matter of culture.

Tim's longer definition says:

"Psychological safety is a social condition in which you feel:

- Included

- Safe to learn

- Safe to contribute

- Safe to challenge the status quo

. . . all without fear of being embarrassed, marginalized, or punished in some way."

Those four bullet points are what he calls *The 4 Stages of Psychological Safety* (and I highly recommend Tim's book of that title). At the highest levels of psychological safety, we feel safe to challenge the status quo, all of which leads to a culture of innovation and success.

Saying things like "I don't know how to do this" or "I could be wrong" are prime examples of behaviors that must be modeled and rewarded by leaders, in addition to admitting mistakes. Doing so consistently creates the conditions for others to feel safe enough to follow their lead, and it's far more effective than cajoling people to "be more vulnerable" or to "be brave." When people feel safe asking questions about how to do their work, many mistakes are prevented.

Anonymous surveys can measure the overall feeling of psychological safety in a team and how that might vary across different teams. Measurement can help us gauge the progress that results, not from training and education alone, but from behaviors.

Billy Taylor is a retired Goodyear executive and author of *The Winning Link*. He says, "When people can't show up as their authentic selves, or they're shut down, you don't have a culture of innovation. You have a culture of broken people just coming in to check a box, get their paycheck, and go home."[47] That's not the formula for winning. He adds, "Your best and brightest might tend to hold back if you don't have a method to create that safe space. You're not going to get their best ideas."

ENSURE IT'S ACTUALLY A "SAFE SPACE"

Nika Kabiri, PhD, a University of Washington faculty member in the department of communication, wrote *Money Off the Table: Decision Science and the Secret to Smarter Investing*. In her book, Nika recalled how her manager once addressed a company group after an employee-satisfaction survey produced mixed results. "This is a safe space. We are all being open and vulnerable," her manager said. Nika was asked specifically what could be done to improve.[48]

Even though she was terrified, Nika responded, "You're my manager. I need your feedback or approval to do certain things. And when I reach out to you, you don't respond." This turned out to be a mistake.

Over the following weeks, Nika's manager punished her candor. Nika was constantly reminded how busy the manager was and that she was making a big deal out of nothing. The manager piled on and told Nika she was naive and didn't understand how things worked, chewing her out for not being able to manage herself.

Yikes. You wouldn't blame her for returning to her old habit of not speaking up.

Instead of blaming her manager, Nika thought about what she could do differently next time. She could choose the safety of staying quiet, but, by doing so, the organization would lose the benefit of her voice and ideas. She could ask if she was risking harm by *not* saying anything. What if she had chosen to give feedback privately? To be fair, Nika was put on the spot and didn't have much time to think through her decision. She could be kind to herself about her decision, reflect on her decision, and move forward. And sometimes, we move forward to a new job that we hope has a better culture.

Instead of talking about a "safe space," you might want to realize it's not the space that's safe—it's the people. Each person decides how safe they feel, given the behavior of their leaders and colleagues. Instead of encouraging people to feel safe, eliminate the causes of fear.

SET THE EXAMPLE AS THE LEADER

Kelly Cutchin is the United States country manager for Moneycorp, a London-based international-payments fintech company that provides payment products and services. She recalled a business dinner where her CEO asked everybody a question similar to mine: "What's your biggest mistake?"[49]

Her CEO shared that, while at Mars Corporation, he accidentally pressed a button that shut down the production of blue M&Ms, at a substantial cost to the business.

Kelly followed her CEO's lead and told a story about working as a server during high school. One day, she pushed the hostess aside to answer a customer who walked in and asked, "Is your menu a la carte?"

Kelly said, enthusiastically, "Actually, no. Not everything is served with ice cream."

Through that mistake, she learned the difference between *a la carte* and *a la mode*.

Kelly also learned two things from that dinner discussion:

- You don't need to know everything

- Somebody else has probably made a bigger mistake than you

In a culture with high degrees of psychological safety, you aren't punished for asking questions, saying "I don't know," or being wrong. Feeling safe to learn means feeling safe to make and admit mistakes. Her CEO modeled that behavior for the team, rewarding those who followed his lead to share their own stories.

INVITE YOUR LEADERS TO GO FIRST

Sabrina Malter's career spanned more than 25 years with a pharmaceutical company in Germany. Before retiring to become a consultant, Sabrina was inspired as a listener of *My Favorite Mistake* to ask a question of her new leader at a town-hall meeting.[50]

She asked him, "What's your favorite mistake?" with the intent of connecting everybody to him in a more personal way, since most people were asking technical questions. Sabrina hoped to help normalize the practice of admitting and sharing mistakes.

Her new leader shared a personal story about extending a business trip to include one more meeting, which left his children feeling rejected.

The mistake reminded him to prioritize family. Sharing that story set an example for everybody there—that it was OK to admit mistakes and that it's acceptable to prioritize family over work. He modeled a vulnerable act, and he now had a chance to reward others for doing the same.

PSYCHOLOGICAL SAFETY DRIVES BETTER PERFORMANCE

If an organization's primary objective is avoiding any and all mistakes, people will be unwilling to try anything new, which will prevent them from learning. They will be too fearful to bring forward ideas for improvement or innovation. Punishing mistakes drives them underground, making them cautious and harming the organization's competitiveness.

Amy Edmondson's research shows: "The level of psychological safety on a team is the central measure of that team's culture, health, and vitality."

Notice that she said "team," not "company," as the level of psychological safety will vary across any large and complex organization, given the variation in how the leaders of different teams behave. And some people within a team might feel safer than others.

Edmondson says, "Catching, correcting, and reducing errors are team activities, and if your teams don't have the interpersonal climate they need to do that, then it won't happen."

Her research has shown the positive impact of psychological safety in healthcare, noting that teams with higher levels of psychological safety reported *higher* numbers of errors and patient harm. Wait, isn't that bad? It might be counterintuitive, but those teams didn't *make* more mistakes; they felt safer *admitting* them. That increases their chances of learning from mistakes in ways that help them learn and make adjustments that prevent repeats. People on these teams also have higher job satisfaction and are more engaged in improvement and innovation.

Edmondson says research conducted at Google "put psychological safety on the map" in modern times, as she recalls.[51] *Project Aristotle* aimed to understand why certain teams outperformed others. The answer wasn't the level of education, the diversity in a team, or other factors. The level of psychological safety emerged as the crucial factor. Because there was a high degree of variance across teams, psychological safety could be identified as a key variable across Google.

Psychological safety doesn't just appear. It's the outcome of what we do and how we do it (more so than what we say). I've seen instances where leaders talking about psychological safety, without taking the right actions, actually made things worse. Why? If expectations are raised, it reduces people's tolerance for leaders who continue to marginalize or punish them for speaking up.

Edmondson shares five actions that leaders can take to build psychological safety:

1. "Frame the work as a learning problem, not an execution problem"

2. "Acknowledge your own fallibility"

3. "Model curiosity, and ask lots of questions"

4. "Solicit input and opinions from the group"

5. "Share information about personal- and work-style preferences, and encourage others to do the same"[52]

Cultivating a culture of learning from mistakes alone doesn't guarantee high performance, but Clark teaches us that doing so is a stepping stone toward the highest levels of psychological safety, which results in benefits, including:

- More employee engagement

- Greater employee retention

- More innovation

- Greater success

PULL THE "ANDON CORD" TO REPORT PROBLEMS

Psychological safety isn't just some squishy concept. Nor is it merely a nice way to treat people. It's also a primary driver of Toyota's success. In the book *Toyota Culture*, Jeff Liker (who has studied Toyota for decades) and Mike Hoseus (a former Toyota leader) state plainly that at Toyota, "Mistakes are okay as long as people learn from them."

They add, "[Toyota believes] people must be treated fairly; they must feel psychologically and physically safe . . ." Learning from mistakes requires mutual trust; as Liker and Hoseus write, "Without trust in their employers, employees are reluctant to admit to the existence of problems and learn that it is safest to hide them."[53]

Toyota factories are known for their "andon cord" practices, where any assembly-team member can reach up and pull a cord whenever they see a problem or make a mistake. Within seconds, a team leader is there to provide support and problem-solving. Hoseus describes the first time he accidentally scratched a car on a Toyota assembly line in Japan:

"My first reaction was to let it go. No one would probably see the scratch anyway, and no one would know that I made it. But my conscience got the best of me, and I wanted to see if they really meant what they said about admitting mistakes. So, I pulled the andon, and the team leader came to fix the problem." Hoseus was given a helpful tip about how to hold his air gun in a way that was less likely for it to slip from his hand, which had caused the scratch. Hoseus recalls the team leader "did not seem angry at me for making the scratch."

Taking it one step further, at the afternoon group meeting, Hoseus thought the Japanese were calling him out for the mistake in front of others, but was surprised to see the entire group clapping and smiling, as they all shook his hand or patted him on the back. He confirmed through his interpreter that "They were applauding me because I made a mistake, and I admitted it. I felt like a million bucks, and guess what I did the next time I made a mistake?"[54]

Other organizations, including those in healthcare, can apply the andon concept, providing ways for employees to report problems even if they're not on the assembly line and they don't have a physical cord to pull.

For example, Virginia Mason Medical Center created its "Patient Safety Alert" based on learning from companies like Toyota and Boeing. It works toward a culture where people feel safe to speak up about problems and have mechanisms for doing so, including a hotline to call if they're being ignored or punished for speaking up in their workspace. The number of reported mistakes increased before VMMC could make improvements that drove down mistakes and harm, which also led to lower malpractice insurance rates.

During a 2018 visit to a hospital near Nagoya, Japan, that had been coached by Toyota, a physician shared a chart that showed an increase in the number of patient-safety incidents reported in recent years. Hospital leaders believed that the number of actual incidents was not increasing—just the reports of them, as people felt safer speaking up. As her slide said, "The primary purpose of patient-safety reporting systems is to learn from experience. A reporting system must produce a visible, useful response . . . to stimulate reporting."

Competing automakers have made the mistake of copying the tool (the physical andon-cord system) while assuming it will work as well without a Toyota-like culture. I remember a 2007 BBC story about a new Ford assembly plant, in Michigan, where the andon cords were being pulled only twice a week.[55] If you visit a Toyota plant, you see and hear the evidence of andon cords being pulled (blinking lights and musical tones) almost constantly—2000 times a day per that article. Seeds of helpful tools won't grow when planted into infertile soil.

People won't speak up or reach up to pull the cord (or call that hotline) in workplaces with low levels of psychological safety and leaders who react horribly to bad news. Problems get repeated. Morale and quality suffer. And in healthcare, patients suffer. And die.

Toyota is well known for its "respect for people" principles and its commitment to the physical safety of employees. Again, from Liker and Hoseus: "Safety [at Toyota] includes more than just physical safety; it also means feeling safe psychologically."

Psychological safety leads to continuous improvement and innovation in a Toyota culture "that involves the ideas and input of all the members to create positive results in which all can take pride."

MANAGEMENT CHANGE LEADS TO CULTURE CHANGE

Isao Yoshino retired in the early 2000s after a 40-year career with Toyota, full of growth through successes and failures. In the early 1980s, Yoshino was responsible for training American frontline managers hired by the "NUMMI" factory in Fremont, California, when it was first established as a joint venture between Toyota and General Motors.[56]

NUMMI is a great illustration of the positive impact of Toyota's culture and leadership style on performance. GM had shut down the original Fremont factory in 1982 after a long track record of terrible productivity and quality. It was one of GM's worst performers. Buyers of GM Fremont vehicles complained about rattling noises, for example, a problem sometimes caused by manufacturing mistakes. But GM Fremont workers sometimes put bolts or empty soda cans inside door panels as an act of sabotage, lashing out against managers and a company they hated.[57]

Working at a Michigan GM plant in 1995, I suffered through the GM tradition of managers blaming workers for quality problems and poor results. A sign of a strong corporate culture is experiencing the same things across disparate locations and decades. GM didn't have a worker problem; it was a management problem.

When NUMMI started production in 1984, 80% of the team members hired came from the UAW pool of workers laid off by GM Fremont. In fact, the UAW still represented the workers. Same building, same workers, same union, but under new management. It was a joint venture, but all of the senior leaders were from Toyota, using a copy of the Toyota Production System.[58]

Within a year, Toyota's management principles and practices boosted NUMMI to the top of the auto industry's quality and productivity rankings. By the fall of 1986, quality and productivity nearly matched one of Toyota's Japanese plants, and GM leaders praised the "excellent labor relations."[59] The lesson was clear: the same workers who had previously failed under GM management were able to thrive under Toyota's leadership.

Case in point: the GM Livonia Engine Plant, where I started my career, was turned around by a new plant manager—a GM lifer, Larry Spiegel, who had been sent to NUMMI to learn from Toyota. In 1996, I remember Larry telling all 800 employees that the era of blaming workers had ended in our plant, and we would succeed together as a result of a different management approach. He was correct, as the plant rose from "the worst of the worst" to the top quartile of GM plants within a few years.

Another one of the first GM people sent to NUMMI was Gary Convis. Unlike Larry, he left to join Toyota, retiring in 2007 as head of Toyota engineering and manufacturing in North America. He explained a core mindset: "You respect people, you listen to them, and you work together. You don't blame them. Maybe the process was not set up well, so it was easy to make a mistake."

FEELING SAFE TO LEARN FROM MISTAKES AT TOYOTA

Did Yoshino make mistakes? Of course. He says, "I've made so many mistakes in my entire life . . . big and small!"

When Yoshino joined Toyota fresh out of university in 1966, his four-month orientation included multiple weeks in a factory's paint shop. Part of Yoshino's job was to add paint and solvent to a machine that mixed them and fed the paint sprayers every two to three hours.

During his first week, assembly workers saw a major problem. The paint wasn't sticking properly to vehicle body panels, meaning at least 100 cars had to be repainted. Yoshino learned this when a group entered the paint shop, shouting about the problem. He remembers feeling sick and thinking, "I must have done something wrong." Yoshino's managers asked him to show them the process by which he poured the cans into the tank.

They discovered that Yoshino had poured an incorrect solvent into the tank. As a young employee, he was surprised by the way the organization responded. It was immediately obvious that the cans looked identical, and it was easy to mix them up. The correct solvent didn't have a defined storage location. It was a systemic problem.

Beyond not blaming Yoshino for the mistake, his managers *thanked* him for making it, explaining that the problem was *management's* mistake for not setting up a newcomer to be successful. They would work together to improve the process immediately so that Yoshino (and other employees) couldn't add the wrong solvent.

Yoshino recalls talking to other new employees in the orientation program, who worked in a different department. They had all made similar mistakes and encountered the same non-blaming problem-solving reaction. That points to a consistent culture. Yoshino said, "You cannot get anything out of blaming somebody," a management lesson that became the foundation for the leader he wanted to become.

The experience made Yoshino happy and taught him important mindsets that he uses to this day:

- Learn from mistakes

- Remember that people are not perfect

- We all make mistakes

- Mistakes happen everywhere (particularly with new employees)

Since he wasn't aware that he was adding the wrong solvent, Yoshino wasn't in a position to speak up about the mistake. It wasn't a matter of feeling safe to speak up or not. He didn't actually *know* that he had made a mistake. When the resulting paint problem was visible, his manager's blame-free reaction created the foundation for him to feel safe to speak up about mistakes in future settings and about how he wanted to respond to others if he was in the same position to discover them.

WHAT IF TOYOTA RAN A HOSPITAL?

What would we expect to have happened in Dr. David Mayer's story if he worked in a hospital with a culture of learning from mistakes? Without the fear of punishment, the attending and resident surgeons, along with David as the resident anesthesiologist, would have more likely felt safe telling the truth to the patient and administrators, unless perhaps pride or embarrassment got in the way.

A Toyota-like hospital would have learned from the mistake, helping those involved participate in problem-solving and prevention instead of feeling relief (and guilt) over getting away with the mistake and deception. The hospital could learn from the relatively minor mistake, improving processes and systems in ways that could prevent other wrong-side or wrong-site surgeries that might have resulted in lasting harm to a patient.

Without the opportunity and ability to learn from mistakes, we are doomed to repeat them.

David's patient wasn't gravely harmed by the hernia-procedure mistake, although an unnecessary incision increases the risk of infection. Even a "near miss" situation, where a surgeon *almost* made the incision on the wrong side, should be seen as an opportunity for improvement, not a time to say "whew" before moving on. We need everybody in the operating room to feel safe reporting near-mistakes in a way that leads to improvement and prevention. And we should all feel that safety in any workplace.

If Toyota ran the hospital, it's quite possible that David wouldn't have had a story to inspire him and others. They would have learned from any previous incidents, including events that cause harm and near-misses. A system designed with proper mistake-proofing would likely have prevented that type of mishap from ever occurring.

For one, a Toyota surgical team would consistently follow current best practices: the surgeon would mark [where the incision should go] near the surgical site, while the patient was still awake to confirm, in the pre-op prep room. They would properly complete the time-out and the rest of the universal protocol (meaning not just going through the motions) before an incision was made, fully confirming the correct patient, procedure, and side. If a surgeon tried circumventing the mistake-proofing steps, any team member would have the ability to "stop the line" without fear of retribution.

A culture of learning from mistakes combines the methods as an integrated system. We first use effective mistake-proofing methods, as discussed in Chapter Four. Leaders act in ways that create conditions where people feel safe to admit mistakes that still occur, as discussed in this chapter. Additionally, leaders must react calmly, without blame or punishment (Chapter Six), collaborating to solve problems and prevent mistakes from being repeated (Chapter Seven).

We need to reduce not just the *fear* factor but also the *futility* factor.

CHAPTER SIX

CHOOSE IMPROVEMENT, NOT PUNISHMENT

"When I make a mistake, I have eight different people
coming by to tell me about it. That's my only real motivation:
not to be hassled. That and the fear of losing my job."
"But you know, Bob, that will only make someone
work just hard enough not to get fired."

—PETER GIBBONS

in the movie *Office Space*

W hen I started my career at General Motors in 1995, it was an old-school environment. Call me naive, but I was shocked to see leaders yelling at people about poor results, even when these were not caused by a mistake. In modern-day healthcare, punitive responses are so prevalent that the same description gets used very widely: "naming, blaming, and shaming." That fact that it rhymes doesn't make it cute. Or effective.

Peter Gibbons faced subtle and mildly passive-aggressive punishment at Innitech, his company in *Office Space*. Nobody

109

yelled. But his leaders were far from helpful. When Peter forgot to attach one of the new cover sheets to his "TPS Report," his vice president, Bill Lumbergh, stopped by to point out the mistake. Peter said, "Yeah, I forgot." It was a "slip," not a knowledge gap.

As if he didn't hear him, Bill droned on, telling Peter to use the new cover sheets. Peter acknowledged he knows to do this. He'd received the memo about the change, and it was still sitting on his desk. Bill cluelessly added that he would send another copy.

Shortly after, another manager, Dom, walked over to calmly tell Peter about the same problem. Peter again explained, "The problem is just I forgot the one time." Dom also reiterated what Peter already acknowledged knowing, telling Peter to "try to remember to do that from now on," punctuated with "That would be great." Reminding Peter not to forget doesn't count as mistake-proofing.

While Innitech certainly didn't seem to have a culture with high psychological safety, Peter nonetheless felt comfortable admitting his mistake at the time. He owned it. While the fictional Innitech's need is made clear, all real organizations need leaders to be constructive when mistakes are made or discovered. Not just calm or polite, but helpful. Effective problem-solving helps everybody avoid repeating mistakes. And engaging people in that effort sets the stage for even greater improvement and innovation.

I greatly appreciate when others react kindly to my mistakes, as it helps me focus on improving my work instead of shaming myself. While preparing for the episode with Jim McCann, the Founder and Chairman of 1-800-FLOWERS, I sent his team the wrong date before correcting it in a new message. I was afraid his team would think I was a flake or that they'd wonder if it was a mistake to put Jim on my podcast. I felt embarrassed.

After the episode, I apologized to Jim for any confusion or inconvenience. Jim shrugged it off and said with a big laugh, "As they say in the old country, it doesn't matter!" His good-natured response sets a good example. But it doesn't help me to prevent repeating the mistake. I needed to figure out how to prevent repeating this mistake with another guest.

Normally, my guests (or their representatives) schedule episodes using an online form, which automatically sends an email and a calendar invitation with the correct date, time, and time zone. In Jim's case, I wanted to save him some time, so I bypassed my usual process by manually sending an email with information about where, when, and how we would record the episode, which created the opportunity for my mistake, ironically taking up more of Jim's time with my rework. A better way to save time for guests like Jim is my new practice of filling out my booking form on their behalf, keeping my usual automated-process steps in place, reducing the risk of mistakes.

In Chapter Four, I mentioned the incredibly gracious response from my guest that one time I forgot to click "Record." Recently, I experienced the same mistake, this time as a guest on someone else's podcast. I reminded myself to follow the example set by my guest when it was my mistake, using similar words to reply, "It's OK. Let's call it a *practice session*. We'll do it again."

Our willingness to learn from mistakes, to choose improvement over punishment, doesn't give people permission to be reckless. Psychological safety, learning, and problem-solving is the pathway to fewer mistakes. Punishment won't get us there.

Leaders can acknowledge when a mistake has a negative impact on a customer or our organization. We can contain the problem, apologize, and mitigate the immediate impact. My wife, as an executive, often tells people, "What happened is bad. But what can we learn and do to ensure it doesn't happen again?"

YELLING AT SOMEBODY DOESN'T MAKE THEM LESS LIKELY TO REPEAT THE MISTAKE

Career coach Jason Levin is the author of *Relationships to Infinity: The Art and Science of Keeping in Touch*. As a student at Rowan University, formerly Glassboro State College, Jason was elected student-government president. Jason was asked to meet with Henry Rowan, whose $100 million donation led to renaming the school after him.

Jason makes no excuses. He scheduled a meeting, but when the initial time no longer worked for him, Jason lost track of the need to reschedule. It slipped his mind. He learned of his mistake two weeks later, when the vice president of institutional advancement called Jason into his office and yelled at him for half an hour.

"I was ready to leave after a minute," Jason recalls about being completely dressed down. The VP kept asking, "What were you thinking?" and set a clear expectation that Jason needed to follow up. Like Peter Gibbons, Jason already knew this.

Jason recovered from the missteps with Rowan (the man and the school). He learned he needed to get better at following through on his responsibilities and that a simple notepad could do the trick. It's a lesson he has carried with him in his career.

Jason learned to appreciate that feedback is a gift. But yelling and screaming for 30 minutes might not be the only way—or the best way—to give such a gift.

DEMONSTRATING A MORE CONSTRUCTIVE WAY AT KAINEXUS

Austin, a customer-success manager at KaiNexus, is appreciative of his colleagues' reaction to a recent mistake. As he said in a weekly company meeting, "Everybody showed such grace. Everybody jumped in to help."

At a customer's request, Austin had changed one of the templates they use in the KaiNexus software platform. Two weeks later, one of the lead users from that customer noticed that the template was now missing one of the necessary fields and reached out to Austin for help. Austin realized that he had made a mistake. "I was trying to do it too quickly and didn't double-check my work," he recalls. It's OK. We all make mistakes, especially when under time pressure or otherwise rushing our work.

Austin reached out to the KaiNexus solutions-engineering team, explaining that he had caused the problem. He felt bad and feared there wouldn't be an easy fix, resigning himself to the possibility that some customer data would be lost. Magdalen, a solutions engineer, was able to recover some of the data but needed additional help correcting the root cause of the problem. Adam, the principal software architect, diagnosed and fixed the problem within 30 minutes. Neither the mistake nor the impact was as big as Austin feared, as he had merely *renamed* a database field instead of *deleting* it. No customer data was lost.

The biggest takeaway for Austin was how helpful everyone was from the moment he admitted the mistake. Austin believes that, at previous blame-heavy companies, he would have been chewed out. He would have gotten help, but people would have made clear to him it was a burden.

Austin says the lack of punishment in this situation didn't hinder his ability to learn. Even with a good outcome, he was motivated to reflect on the need to slow down and check his work. But it also reinforced that, at KaiNexus, admitting a mistake and asking for help brings a helpful, constructive response.

The same month as Austin's mistake, I made a mistake, and the impact was mitigated by a kind response. Ten minutes before a webinar's scheduled start time, Morgan, my KaiNexus co-presenter, had problems with her computer. Windows had decided to make updates that forced a slow and untimely reboot. She handled the stress well and found a colleague's laptop to use. While we were able to start on time, I got thrown off track due to the scramble. I had failed to set the webinar to start recording automatically, and I forgot to click "Record"—a mental lapse. I lost track of my checklist at a time when I needed it most.

I learned this about 30 seconds into my welcoming remarks, when the other presenter (Greg, the CEO), sent a private Zoom chat message that asked, "Is this being recorded?" Oops! I disclosed the mistake to the audience and clicked "Record." Had Greg yelled at me (which I would never expect), I would have been distracted the rest of the webinar, hurting my performance. But the kindness of his query allowed me to quickly put the mistake behind me. Thanks to the magic of editing, the recording shows no evidence of what went wrong. Morgan is now using a Mac, which has never surprised me with an inopportune update and restart.

THE CONGRESSMAN WHO CHOSE
LEARNING OVER PUNISHMENT

Ken Segel is a co-founder and CEO of Value Capture. Decades ago, Ken started his career in politics, most notably running the overnight "war room" operations during the 1992 Clinton-Gore campaign.

Ken's first job after college, in 1988, was as a congressional aide for U.S. Representative Howard Berman, from California. As an advisor on immigration policy, Ken received the call when a *USA Today* reporter called. Ken asked to speak with the reporter "on background," a commonly used ground rule that would allow Ken to speak more frankly without fear of being quoted with attribution—or so he thought.[60]

Two days later, Ken found the article in his mailbox with the phrase "See me" written by his boss. Ken read the piece for the first time and was dismayed to read a quote directly attributed to him saying that legislation introduced by Sen. Alan Simpson still treated people from whole sections of the world, including Africa, as if they were "the plague, not human beings seeking a better life for their kids." Ken remembers his life passing before his eyes when he read the quote and the note.

Having worked for the Congressman for just a month or two, Ken assumed Rep. Berman would be quite angry and thought he might be fired. "I'd embarrassed my boss and made it harder to work with a key stakeholder," Ken recalls.

Ken scheduled time to see him at the end of the day. Rep. Berman started by asking Ken questions about other issues related to their work. Ken was a little dumbfounded that the *USA Today* story wasn't the first topic of conversation—and didn't seem to be on the agenda at all.

Ken finally held up the clip and asked, "Don't you want to talk about this?"

Rep. Berman asked, "Do you understand why this is problematic?" Of course, Ken did. He explained how he asked the reporter to treat his comments as background. But, perhaps the quote was just "too juicy not to use," Ken now wonders.

The Congressman replied, "All right, forget it. Just learn, and we'll move on. Forget it." Rep. Berman took the clip, crumpled it up, and threw it in the trash.

Why did Rep. Berman respond that way? Ken doesn't know for sure but thinks the Congressman saw himself as a leader who developed people, adding, "Many other members of Congress have a very different leadership style, which is based on a lot of aggression and taking advantage of their authority over others. But [Rep. Berman] quite deliberately chose a different way."

Ken never learned why the reporter quoted him. Either the reporter intentionally violated his request to be used as background, or it was a mistake. Instead of blaming the reporter, he took ownership of his words. Ken realized that what he said was "endlessly defensible, but not constructive." Ken didn't avoid talking with reporters after that incident but learned to be more cautious in what he said.

Ken left politics and began focusing on various aspects of healthcare improvement. As a core aspect of that work, he and the team at Value Capture help health-system leaders improve their organizations' systems of working, managing, and improving, aiming for a goal of zero harm. For Value Capture to fully help their clients "see, solve, and share problems," as Ken describes, the people working in those organizations need to feel safe bringing problems into the open.

Ken points to two deeper lessons for leaders from his experience with Congressman Berman. First, leaders make the biggest difference for their people when they avoid reacting with blame in the moments when it's hardest not to—when something has gone wrong that puts the leader and the organization under pressure.

Second, when leaders extend forgiveness or safety in the way Congressman Berman did—even in extreme moments—the impact is more than an increased willingness to work on solving problems. When that leader behavior is a habit, we see a tremendous surge of energy, alignment, and loyalty—positive forces that can change the performance trajectory of organizations and last a lifetime.

Ken describes this as his favorite mistake because of how the Congressman handled the situation and the way that made him feel included and safe to learn. Ken was "forever with Howard" because of his constructive response.

REACT WELL WHEN BAD NEWS MOVES UP FASTER

In 2018, General Electric named Larry Culp as the first outside CEO in the company's long and storied history. As he discussed on stage at the 2022 Association for Manufacturing Excellence conference, Larry inherited a company culture where he realized messengers were shot for sharing bad news. He said, "I've seen a number of examples over my career where bad news has not traveled fast, and it can be fatal" to an organization.

How did Larry start cultivating a culture where it would be acceptable to share imperfections, challenges, or mistakes? Larry says, "It's largely about how you deal with bad news" as a leader, which means acknowledging the reality of the situation and working on the problems constructively.

Larry encouraged GE employees to bring him "bad news and to bring it fast." Because he recognized the fear factor, Larry knew he would face a moment of truth when somebody stepped up to share bad news. In the language of psychological safety, he would have to reward the vulnerable act of speaking up if he wanted more employees to do the same. Larry said he proved he could "walk that talk, handle bad news, and not shoot messengers."

"Any of us has the opportunity to create that environment where people want to bring forward an issue, knowing they're going to get help" instead of being chastised, Larry says. This means leaders must "go into problem-solving mode both to contain [the problem] and to deal with the root cause."

Larry added, "I just think that it's so much more powerful if you can find it in yourself to reach out for help, to acknowledge [your] own mistakes, and move forward. People respect that. A lot of people engender followership that way." When a CEO like Larry models vulnerable acts, such as admitting a mistake, and rewards those who do the same, it helps create the psychological safety necessary for the entire company to learn from mistakes.

Choose Improvement, Not Punishment

In 2006, Ford Motor Company hired Alan Mulally away from Boeing to be CEO. He inherited a culture where talking about problems was viewed as a sign of weakness, according to his successor, Mark Fields.[61] Fields said that Mulally turned that around, in part by saying that admitting problems was "a sign of strength."

Mulally asked executives to add color-coding to status updates they gave: green if things were going well, yellow if there were known issues, and red, meaning there was a new problem with no known solution. He recalls, "That was very hard for the Ford people, because they just didn't do red." In the first meetings, every update was green, which was not surprising, given the culture. But Mulally noted this was strange, especially given that the company ended the year $17 billion in the red.

Finally, during a regular review meeting, a business unit leader reported a "red" status update for a vehicle-launch plan. Mulally started clapping, rewarding the vulnerability of this leader's admission that something was off-track. Before long, status updates included a mix of all three colors. Mulally says, "At that moment, we all knew that we were going to trust each other" and that they "were going to help each other to turn the reds to yellows to greens." The first to report a red? Mark Fields. Maybe it's not surprising that he succeeded Mulally as CEO.

CELEBRATE MISTAKES AND LEARN

Stephen King (not the famous novelist) is the CEO of GrowthForce, a company that provides accounting and book-keeping services. Stephen says learning from mistakes is the "single most-important part" of their culture.[62]

Stephen wants his employees to feel safe sharing mistakes. One employee admitted she had entered the wrong bank account for a sales-tax payment, resulting in a $2500 late-payment penalty. How does Stephen react to mistakes like these? "By learning from that first mistake, you avoid that down the road. You put a process in place" to prevent or catch mistakes.

Stephen leads the way and models behaviors that help build psychological safety. For example, after a sales call, he asks, "What did I do wrong? How do we make that better?" He adds, "When the boss makes a lot of dumb mistakes, you'd better learn from them." That gives permission for others to admit mistakes. While we might avoid the word "dumb," employees can follow Stephen's lead in learning from mistakes.

He created an award for the "best mistake of the month," meaning it's "one we can fix" and has "the greatest impact on the business." This can surprise new employees, who tell him they've never worked in a place that celebrated mistakes, let alone give a $50 gift card for making one. A few managers pushed back on the financial reward, but learning from mistakes is built into the culture and is now reinforced by giving people recognition instead of rewards.

ACCEPT MISTAKES TO DRIVE BETTER PERFORMANCE

"I'm a big fan of making mistakes", says Bob Rush, who has enjoyed a long career as a leader in manufacturing companies. Being influenced deeply by Toyota and the Lean methodology, Bob says a good culture "sends people home healthy and happy. They shouldn't worry about their jobs or a mistake." He encourages colleagues to help people learn from their mistakes.

Choose Improvement, Not Punishment

Like Stephen King, Bob created a reward for "the biggest mistake" in some of his workplaces. In his experience, "People soon realize that if you could laugh about a mistake, you could tell others about mistakes. If they're comfortable enough to laugh with you, they're comfortable enough to tell you the bad things. Sometimes it takes a while, but you've got to do it. That's part of the culture."

But doesn't rewarding mistakes lead to more mistakes? Bob learned you can identify the small percentage of people who "would try to make a mistake to get the reward." He tells employees, "I'm not looking for you to make mistakes. I want you to *tell me* that you made a mistake." Bob also wants people to propose solutions, so that they can work together on improvement.

Bob says that accepting mistakes doesn't mean accepting bad performance. Accepting the reality of mistakes, instead of denying or hiding them, allows us to focus on improvement, which leads to better performance.

In *Toyota Culture*, Liker and Hoseus say, "Toyota makes mistakes like other companies, but they are better than most at responding and fixing the mistakes."[63] Hoseus also tells a story in the book about building trust with workers in Kentucky. As mentioned in Chapter Five, vehicles being scratched was "a big problem," so, to help encourage team members to pull the andon cord, anybody who did so and admitted a mistake was given a coupon for a free soda in the cafeteria. With the campaign and efforts to build mutual trust, "there was actually a decrease in total scratches over the course of the month" because the safety to speak up was followed by effective problem-solving.

IMPROVE SYSTEMS INSTEAD OF BLAMING INDIVIDUALS

W. Edwards Deming said, "American management is quick to assign blame to an individual when the problem is, in fact, a fault in the system." Unfortunately, this remains true more than 30 years after his passing. Blaming and punishing individuals for systemic errors is not only unfair—it's ineffective. As people learn to protect themselves, they drive mistakes underground in a way that ensures they continue to happen.

In healthcare, this means more patients will be harmed in the future. So, why do healthcare leaders too often make this mistake? Dr. David Mayer believes that "Hospitals find it's the easy way out. If you could blame a nurse for something that any nurse might've done or a physician for a mistake that any physician might've made in the same situation, boom, you 'solved' the problem in your mind." But it's not solved, as he knows.

David has learned that punishing people for mistakes often just leads to "the culture of that hospital being destroyed." He says suspending the nurse or dismissing a physician for making a mistake does not solve the actual cause of the systemic problem. On the other hand, if an individual was recklessly and intentionally flouting safety policies, that might be a time for leaders to "hold them accountable."

When is it appropriate to punish an individual for actions that lead to a bad outcome? It is not helpful to blame individuals for mistakes that have systemic causes. It's counterproductive to punish people for simple human error when management and the system failed the individual by not having effective mistake-proofing in place. Fix the system instead of blaming, punishing, or replacing individuals.

A framework known as "Just Culture" originated in aviation and has started spreading in healthcare. Dr. Lucian Leape, a legendary figure in the patient-safety movement, says, "Approaches that focus on punishing individuals instead of changing systems provide strong incentives for people to report only those errors they cannot hide. Thus, a punitive approach shuts off the information needed to identify faulty systems and create safer ones. In a punitive system, no one learns from their mistakes."

The Just Culture framework provides an algorithm for deciding if a bad outcome was caused by system causes or an individual act, and for distinguishing between human error, at-risk behaviors, and reckless acts. Sometimes misunderstood as a "zero blame" approach, Just Culture helps us determine when it *would* be fair and just to blame an individual. How often? The answer is "Not never, but not often."

In this model, punishment is appropriate only for an intentional act committed by an individual who knew they would cause harm. It's not fair and just to punish an individual for an honest mistake (including the resident who cut into the wrong side). There is some gray area, where "reckless acts," such as performing surgery under the influence of alcohol or drugs, might merit punishment.

Brook Ward, President and CEO of Washington Health System, started implementing the Just Culture concept five years ago. He says it "allows the organization to foster honest admissions of mistakes" since they are not automatically blaming individuals. They are instead "fixing the system issues to assist the team in avoiding mistakes going forward."

Before fixing systemic issues, we should first console the person or people who were involved in a mistake. While we should punish intentional acts, including sabotage and murder, we should take a different approach in situations where there's no conscious choice or intent to do harm. There's a big difference between an honest mistake that leads to the accidental overdose of a patient and a so-called "angel of death" who intentionally ends a patient's life.

Thinking back to the story from Chapter Five, it's unfair to punish the resident surgeon for the wrong-side incision in the hernia-repair case, as it was clearly a mistake. There was no intent. But what about the attending surgeon who made a conscious decision to lie? They probably worked in an environment without much psychological safety. I don't like the decision, but I can understand how the culture influenced that choice.

In a culture where non-punitive reactions were the norm, the surgeon might have felt safe to disclose the mistake to the patient, with an apology. Non-punitive responses must also include effective problem-solving, otherwise, mistakes will continue if we don't eliminate the root causes of mistakes. Don't replace fear with futility.

CREATE SAFE OPPORTUNITIES TO PRACTICE AND LEARN

In Chapter One, KaiNexus co-founder and COO Matt Paliulis described a culture of learning from mistakes. As a web-based software company, one of the biggest risks they face would be an unauthorized incursion into its platform. Hackers try to get in through "phishing" attempts, tempting a KaiNexian to click a nefarious link in an email that looks legitimate. That mistake could jeopardize customer data, if not the future of the company.

To reduce the risk of damage, KaiNexus doesn't rely solely on educating employees about risks and threats. Awareness helps, but they don't hang up a bunch of posters or send Slack messages constantly reminding everyone to be careful.

KaiNexus pays a firm to perform occasional, unannounced "social-engineering-penetration tests." Employees receive emails that might look suspicious to some, but no real harm comes from clicking the "bad" link. The firm also places phone calls to KaiNexians, pretending to be a customer (even using a real customer name).

Instead of just hearing about risks, active testing (and the risk of failing the test) is a more powerful way to learn. The company would rather have somebody make a mistake (and learn) through a test instead of an actual attack.

In these situations, covering up a mistake is more damaging than admitting it, so KaiNexus leaders, including Matt, emphasize that it's safe to admit a mistake—whether one thinks it's a test or not. In a recent company meeting, Matt explained it's safe to come to him if somebody even *suspects* they might have clicked on a dangerous link. He emphasized that prompt reporting protects the company from further damage and won't lead to punishment. Leaders like Matt are committed to acting in ways that are consistent with their words.

MY OPPORTUNITY TO REACT WELL AT KAINEXUS

In March 2021, as part of the KaiNexus webinar series, I was the host of a virtual panel discussion moderated by Deondra

Wardelle, a business coach and strategist. During the Q&A period, we all saw an alarming message pop up on our screens:

"This meeting has been ended by host."

Wait, what? As host, I had done no such thing! I hadn't clicked the wrong button. A few other KaiNexians and I started investigating, trying to figure out "What happened?" and not asking, "Who did that?"

It turns out that another KaiNexian—let's call them "Sam"—had started a Zoom Meeting using the same account that I was using for this Zoom Webinar. Instead of getting upset at Sam, we looked at where our process might have failed.

First, I called Sam for their perspective on what had happened. I remember first asking, "How are you? Are you OK?" Sam replied that they were feeling terrible for ending the webinar. Deondra had already reacted very kindly, writing in an email, "I'm sure the person involved feels horrible. Please let them know I'm not upset. We can classify what happened as an opportunity for learning and improvement."

We learned that the bad outcome was caused by a few systemic problems that lined up against us. For one, Sam hadn't accepted the calendar invitation. Had they done so, Sam would have seen not to schedule a meeting for that same time. Sam's planned countermeasure was to accept those invites in the future, but we knew that wouldn't be perfectly mistake-proofed.

Sam called Zoom technical support to ask why the act of starting a meeting would immediately end a webinar on the same account. Was this a bug, or was it working as intended? Sam suggested that maybe Zoom should give a warning when a user tries to start a meeting while also running a webinar. This could be an *"Are you sure? Another meeting is already in progress"*-type warning that might serve as an imperfect mistake-proofing mechanism.

The Zoom agent reminded Sam there was no need for such a warning because . . . we weren't supposed to share an account. Oof, point taken. Our mistake. My mistake. Sharing the account with Sam was a misguided cost-reduction attempt that turned out not to be worth the risk. And I have to admit, we *were* violating the terms of the Zoom service. We learned our lesson and separated out our Zoom accounts, moving webinar functionality to a Zoom account that would be used only for webinars. Problem solved. Lesson learned. The Zoom Webinars account would never be double-booked again.

In reality, this is a lesson I should have learned several months earlier. The accidental ending of that March 2021 webinar should have been prevented, had I learned the correct lessons at the time of a mistake that happened six months earlier during another webinar.

NOT LEARNING THE CORRECT LESSON
FROM A PRIOR MISTAKE

Our bad decision to use the shared account had caused a different, less-severe, problem for an earlier panel-discussion webinar I hosted in October 2020, which, ironically, was also moderated by Deondra.

A few minutes into the webinar, the very same Sam unexpectedly appeared on screen as an additional panelist. This was a surprise to everybody, including Sam. They hit the "Leave

Meeting" button in a panic, and most people didn't notice. Sam was trying to join as an attendee to watch and listen. But since they were using the shared Zoom account, they became a panelist like me. We were fortunate that Sam didn't click "End Webinar" by mistake.

Being a very minor, if not slightly comical, mistake, I'm sure most people would choose improvement over punishment in this situation. In my conversation with Sam, I went for kind and helpful, not just nice. Sam and I connected after that webinar, with the shared goal of understanding what happened and how we could improve. At that time, Sam's countermeasure was to watch recordings of future webinars instead of joining live. That adjustment did, in fact, prevent Sam from mistakenly joining again as a panelist. It didn't prevent them from ending that later webinar by starting a meeting at the same time.

However, we now realize that the best countermeasure would have been to separate out the Zoom accounts. We should have asked, "What else could go wrong?" in the spirit of FMEA analysis, as mentioned in Chapter Four. Failing to learn properly from the first mistake doomed us to make the second.

INNOVATE, AND LEARN FROM MISTAKES

We'll continue our efforts to prevent mistakes, including updating our checklists. We'll aim to react kindly when mistakes happen, and I was recently tested on this. I was beginning to answer questions after presenting a webinar when a contractor unplugged my home's internet router. It was a mistake, and I don't blame him, since my device doesn't look anything like a typical router. Ironically, the theme of my webinar was learning from mistakes. Ultimately, the mistake was mine, allowing a contractor into my home during the webinar. I should have seen the risk, but I didn't.

Hosting more webinars means more opportunities for mistakes, especially when trying to innovate with new webinar formats and new technologies. As discussed in the next chapter, we should expect (if not celebrate) mistakes when we are trying to innovate. We can learn from mistakes, preferably early and on a small scale, so that we can prevent major failures.

CHAPTER SEVEN

ITERATE YOUR WAY TO SUCCESS

*"The most creative people—and companies—don't have
lower failure rates. They fail faster and cheaper, and perhaps
learn more from their setbacks than their competitors."*

—PROF. BOB SUTTON
Stanford University
Author of books, including
The No Asshole Rule

Chris Bianco is a James Beard award-winning chef and
owner of Pizzeria Bianco, whose wood-oven pizzas are often
named the nation's best. After enjoying his Phoenix restaurant
for years, my wife and I moved to Dallas in 2005, where we
couldn't find a similar pizzeria. I was inspired to start making
pizza in our backyard. We even toyed with the idea of building
a brick oven like Bianco's.

Before committing to the investment, it seemed prudent to
start cooking pizzas on an inexpensive stone I could put on my

gas grill. That doesn't work as well as a wood oven, but it allowed us to test a few assumptions, such as being able to make and stretch dough properly and not getting bored with making (or eating) pizza. After that small test of change, we went all-in on the pizza oven, and I haven't regretted it.

After using the backyard wood oven a few times, I had an opportunity to return to Pizzeria Bianco, where I asked Chris for his advice as a new pizza maker. I'll never forget his answer, in his raspy Brooklyn accent: "Just keep burnin' 'em, 'til you get it right!"

As Chris reminded me, we should expect to make mistakes when we're learning or trying something new. We should also remember that mistakes are possible anytime we try to improve a product or our process. But we can learn from those mistakes and move forward, better.

REPLACE FALSE CERTAINTY WITH LEARNING THROUGH EXPERIMENTS

Professor John Grout observes that his "A students" are "the ones who think they know everything." Knowing and citing facts can earn us top marks in school. But getting too used to being all-knowing can lead students to perform poorly in settings that require the ability to acknowledge and learn from early failures in a way that leads to better results.[64]

For example, in one famed exercise, competing teams are given eighteen minutes to build the tallest structure from twenty sticks of spaghetti, one yard of tape, one yard of string, and one marshmallow.[65] The winning teams are invariably the ones who start building the soonest, using small experiments. They fail, learn, adjust, and eventually win. The losing teams spend the most time talking about solutions before they try building anything, only to learn too late, without enough time left to adjust. Kindergarten students beat MBA students in this exercise because they're more willing to try and fail on a small scale without shame.

Clarity First author Karen Martin laments how executives "crave certainty" about what we know or expect to happen. She says, "It's very unusual to have certainty. I think of certainty as being a form of arrogance because we can't ever be certain. If you can heighten people's sensitivity to the fact they're operating from that mindset, that can free them up to be more hypothesis-based thinkers and experimenters. That's good for everybody."[66]

She adds, "We can be certain once facts are present and you've got a pattern. You can ease your way toward certainty, but you're never fully certain. It's a fallacy that you must get to certainty before doing anything. There's such a corporate mindset of 'It *must* be—it *has* to work.' This pressure for perfection just isn't realistic."

Karen suggests that leaders embrace *thoughtful experimentation based on data*, a far-more intentional state of mind than "throwing spaghetti on the wall to see what sticks."

TEST YOUR IDEAS, AND LEARN

We can learn from small mistakes that just happen, or we can reduce the chance of large mistakes by heading them off with small ones.

Mary Greeley Medical Center, a 220-bed community hospital in Ames, Iowa, received the prestigious Malcolm Baldrige National Quality Award in 2019. CEO Brian Dieter continually emphasizes the necessity to "engage those closest to the work to develop ways to improve their work, and then be willing to let them test these improvements."

One day, when I visited the hospital to facilitate a continuous-improvement workshop, a nurse spoke up about a problem. It was difficult for patients to reach power outlets for charging their phones. Their personal items, like phones and eyeglasses, frequently fell from beds to the floor. Ideally, the patient would press their call button for help, as instructed. But if they wanted to be self-sufficient or didn't get a timely response from the care team, a patient might try retrieving their items, leading to falling and being injured.

The nurse had an idea. He wanted the hospital to buy a small caddy, with pockets and a power outlet, that could be attached to each patient's bedrail. The expected outcome would be the number of call-light signals for dropped items decreasing, if not going to zero. It seemed reasonable but needed to be confirmed in real use.

At $20 each, it would cost $4,400 to buy one for each bed. As I had learned from my mentors, I asked, as gently as possible, "What's the smallest test of change we could try first?"

"One unit," the nurse replied, meaning all the beds in one unit. I blurted out, "Is that the *smallest* possible test of change?"

"Oh, one bed!" he said, thankfully, with a smile.

We didn't want to overthink the situation. Still, we discussed the differences between what we *knew* to be a fact and what was merely a hypothesis or an assumption.

For example, would patients use them? We hoped so. If used, how well would they work? Did we know which of the caddies in the catalog worked best? No. Did we know which was the most cost-effective or most durable over time? We didn't know. Would this "countermeasure" potentially create new risks if they were difficult to disinfect between patients? Had we considered other countermeasures?

Turning a hypothesis into knowledge required testing at least one caddy. Buying a few different caddies to test in parallel for $100 would be better than potentially making a mistake costing forty times more.

They proceeded with this pilot, observed patients using the caddies, and asked them for feedback. Starting with one patient didn't mean a final decision would be appropriate after a single test. The team might decide to continue trials with different patients, increasing the size of trials in a way that would be less expensive and less risky than jumping to buy 220 of them.

The hospital realized that the pilot could have a number of outcomes. They might end up choosing the best caddy to purchase for all beds. Or they might learn that different caddies work better in various units or with different types of patients. The initial hypothesis of buying the same caddy for all beds might be incorrect, and that would be OK.

If an experiment doesn't pan out, it's easier for people to admit it when the cost of testing it is small. Scientific improvement means we're open to having our hypothesis disproved, through data, instead of trying to convince everybody we were right.

The hospital decided not to buy caddies for all beds, but each inpatient unit was given the option to purchase and use them.

CEO Brian Dieter adds that improvement is "direction, not a destination" and "having 1400 employees looking for small changes every day is how the hospital will achieve our vision of 'being the best.'"

BE HUMBLE, NOT STUBBORN

Toyota's core-management mindsets include leading with humility. Darril Wilburn and Sammy Obara, both formerly of Toyota, might have told the people at Mary Greeley this: "Humility says that we don't really know, so we must understand and then try many things to see if we have the right solution. If not, we try again."[67]

Taiichi Ohno, one of the creators of the Toyota Production System, wrote: "It is not good if you hold on to your ideas too strongly and try stubbornly to justify them. We are all human, and we are wrong half of the time."

It would be a mistake to take the word "half" literally in that last sentence. We don't know that we're wrong half the time or even close to that. But we certainly have two possibilities every time we make a decision: we could be right, or we could be wrong. My mistake. There are more than two possibilities, as we could be somewhat wrong. Assuming we are right is far more dangerous than knowing we could be wrong.

When we prepare to test a countermeasure, saying, "I could be wrong" remains a compelling statement. It's more important for senior leaders to believe and say this. Inviting others to challenge our ideas can strengthen our hypothesis in a way that reduces our chances of making a mistake.

DON'T JUST PLAN AND DO, ALSO STUDY AND ADJUST

When starting with a small test of change, we should expect the possibility of being wrong. Many organizations think about implementing solutions as a fixed, linear path: We have an idea; we implement it. We know it will be successful. In contrast, Toyota fully embraces the mindset of "Plan, Do, Study, Adjust" or "PDSA," often called the "Deming Cycle" after W. Edwards Deming, PhD.

We don't just plan, do, and assume our idea is a good one that will work out as expected, without a doubt. PDSA is a cycle, or a series of cycles, that moves us closer to our goal in an iterative way.

In a PDSA cycle, we "Plan" our tests based on gaining a solid understanding of our problem and situation. After we "Do" something, thinking of it as a test, we need to "Study" the effect (comparing the actual outcome to our hypothesis). We can "Adjust" (if needed) based on what we've learned. If we didn't get the results we expected, we might need to make some major adjustments to our approach.

As Jeff Liker, author of *The Toyota Way* series of books, told me, Toyota encourages experimentation. If you have an idea, they are less likely to debate it and more likely to say, "Please try it, and you will learn." A "failed experiment" is seen as a hypothesis that was not supported, not a mistake in the sense that an individual or a team has failed.

But even if our small test gave us the results we'd predicted (or better), we can still make small adjustments to improve upon our improvement, testing those in a new cycle. And the iteration continues as we approach our ideal state and ultimate goal (such as zero harm or 100% customer satisfaction).

FAILURES ARE INFORMATION

Problem-solving expert Melanie Parrish is the author of *The Experimental Leader: Be a New Kind of Boss to Cultivate an Organization of Innovators*.[68] To her, an experiment is a mistake only if you pursue it for so long that you spend more money than you can afford to lose.

She says, "The first way to become an experimental leader is to start using the language of experimentation. We're going to have a hypothesis. We're going to test that hypothesis. And then we're going to make decisions based on that hypothesis." If you think you know the answer, you're probably wrong. "Unless you collect the data, you are just guessing," Melanie adds.

An experimentalist's mind must "almost be a blank slate, so that you are listening more, taking in information," and being prepared to adjust based on data. When you come in with "a preconceived notion of what you want, that really gets in the way of leading toward innovation." She agrees that small mistakes can prevent big mistakes. "If you're experimenting well, failures are just information."

Melanie iterated her way through the writing and publication of her book (as I have been doing here). She says the book she wrote wasn't the one she started to write, and it's better. Like me, she had great editors and collaborators along the way who helped her flesh out ideas by asking hard questions along the way. Her thoughts evolved as she wrote the book, and she loved that process.

THE THERAPIST'S SMALL TEST PREVENTED
AN EXPENSIVE MISTAKE

Mental-health professional Emily Learing is the author of *Henry Knows Best!: A Story About Learning From Mistakes and Listening to Others.* Like the other "official book of the podcast," *The Girl Who Never Made Mistakes,* her children's book provides many helpful reminders to adults.[69] In her book, Henry, a strong-willed Corgi, believes he knows all the answers and that only his way is best. This mindset was not the root cause of Emily's favorite mistake.

As a first-time entrepreneur, Emily started a childcare program she specially designed for children with behavioral challenges and their caregivers, who needed resources and support. She quickly learned that demand was strong for a typical childcare program. Her phone rang off the hook, but it wasn't ideal clients who were calling. Emily shut down the program, but the experience led to conference-speaking invitations that raised her profile and helped her career.

Although it failed, Emily avoided a larger, more-expensive mistake. Emily had mitigated her risk by starting with home-based childcare instead of jumping right to a commercial lease. If the business had grown beyond her home's capacity, she would have been more confident about committing to pay for a dedicated facility. Her small test of change prevented the expensive mistake of being locked into a lease, which would have pressured her to compromise her vision just to pay the rent.

Did she make a mistake by giving up too quickly on her concept? She says, "I probably would've figured things out and been in line with my professional goals," but she moved on.

Later, Emily started her current private practice, Encompass Mental Health, in South Dakota. In her introductory video on its website, Emily explains clearly to prospective clients and employees, "I'm not perfect." She sells her workplace culture to prospective employees by emphasizing, "We're willing to admit when we're wrong." She sets a great example for patients, parents, and colleagues.

Given a choice, be like Emily—not like Henry!

SHIFT FROM "I KNOW I'M RIGHT" TO "I COULD BE WRONG"

I've focused on saying these phrases more often, so I was happy to hear entrepreneur Joel Trammell say, "The two most powerful phrases that CEOs need to use are 'I don't know' and 'I made a mistake.' You could spend a year with some CEOs, and they'd never utter either of those phrases. A lot of CEOs think they have to have all the answers."[70]

Joel wants colleagues to think of him as authentic and transparent. But he says that people won't view you that way "if you're covering up your mistakes and acting like you know everything, when you know you don't."

Testing ideas requires the humility to admit that we might be wrong, or just partially correct. Entrepreneur Jeff Gothelf, author of books, including *Sense and Respond*, *Lean UX*, and *Lean versus Agile versus Design*, says, "Humility is not the abdication of vision or leadership. Humility simply means that, while you may have strong opinions, based on your experience and your expertise, you're willing to change your mind in the face of evidence." This means being willing to admit it when the market refutes your idea, he says.[71]

Jeff adds, "If there is one magic ingredient to make this mindset shift stick, it's humility. And entrepreneurs aren't exactly known for having tons of humility. I think those who do are the ones that ultimately succeed. It's an interesting combination of having enough ego to go and take the risk of starting something, yet having enough humility to learn from what you're doing. That's a unique combination."

Karen Hold is a Procter & Gamble alum, entrepreneur, and author of the book *Experiencing Design: The Innovator's Journey.* She has learned that expecting to be wrong means we should "go out, test assumptions, and find out what has to be true for the idea to be really good. And then you will get closer to success."[72]

She adds, "By making those small bets frequently, you can test your way to success. We need to test because innovators tend to equate being smart with being right, and that's not the case in innovation. It's hard for them to believe they're "going to get it wrong most of the time." If we don't believe we can get it wrong, we won't be ready to learn and iterate.

Karen reminds us that the best investors in Silicon Valley are "right" only about two times out of ten. She says we should extend that same expectation to our innovation efforts, reminding us that always getting it right is an unrealistic goal.

Additionally, entrepreneur and consultant Andrea Jones values the opportunity to learn over being convinced she's right. "I think that life is about trying things and recognizing that they're not always going to turn out how you thought they would," she said.

Andrea emphasizes the need to admit and accept the reality of a mistake. And if we can "accept some level of blame as a leader, almost to a fault, then everybody will be much more open to having a productive conversation about what happened when they're not blamed."

Because life is constantly changing, "We get to experiment. We get to make these mistakes. We get to try again. And if leaders can admit that and show that level of vulnerability, everybody will get there much faster. And I love that."[73] Recognizing and admitting mistakes means more improvement, growth, and success.

YOU CAN'T HAVE ALL THE ANSWERS

Pamela Kellert is a coach for women in STEM careers. In her first manager role, she thought she needed to know all the answers. Leaders can learn from that mistake by adjusting to a more-humble mindset and leadership style. They're more likely to make that adjustment when they work for senior leaders who admit they could be wrong, or that they were.[74]

One leader who navigated this transition was John Toussaint, MD, formerly CEO of the ThedaCare health system. Now a coach to healthcare CEOs, he emphasizes his own progression from being an "all-knowing leader" who made many top-down decisions, to a leader who guides and facilitates, one who helps others get better at problem-solving and improvement.[75] As CEO, John learned from some of his board members, particularly CEOs of companies that practiced Toyota-based Lean Management approaches.

That's why I've worked to develop a habit of saying, "I might be wrong." I try saying it as often as possible, not out of a sense of false modesty, but acknowledging (to myself and others) the difference between what I *know* to be true and what I *suspect* to be true. Mentors of mine, formerly of Toyota, would often ask an essential question in response when they heard what sounds like a fact: "How do you know that to be true?" They'd ask, "What do you know? And how do you know it?"

With an "I could be wrong" (or "I might not be completely correct") mindset, we're more open to adjusting based on feedback and data. This mitigates the risk of a bad decision, as we can pivot away from it instead of doubling down. Are we prepared to be proven wrong, or do we just want to be proven right?

If the creator of a new product or service is convinced they're right, failing to listen to the concerns of others can result in big mistakes and failures. And this is especially true if you're the CEO or another leader in a position of power. Can you remember the last time an employee of yours challenged something you said or one of your ideas? If not, you have a problem. Unless you cultivate an environment where people feel safe to disagree, you'll make many unnecessary mistakes.

REACTING CONSTRUCTIVELY TO A MISTAKE WAS A HUGE VICTORY FOR GARRISON BROTHERS DISTILLERY

I think companies that react constructively to mistakes are better positioned to turn a mistake into something positive. Today, Garrison Brothers Distillery produces award-winning Bourbon from Texas white corn (along with other Texas-grown grains, including wheat and barley). When he started, Dan Garrison used yellow corn, since that was the norm for Kentucky Bourbon, even if his choice of organic, food-grade corn was innovative.

One day, as described in the book *Texas Whiskey*, a truckload of the wrong corn ("Texas #1 Panhandle White Corn") pulled up unexpectedly at the distillery. As Dan told me, "When you're in startup mode, anything free is a Godsend."

Dan asked his Kentucky distilling mentors for advice, and they said that changing the type of corn would not have any effect on the Bourbon after aging for five years. If the white corn was basically interchangeable with the yellow corn, then using it wouldn't create any risk of failure.

In the first experiment, the white corn yielded a higher level of sugar than the yellow corn, which meant more food for yeast to convert to alcohol. Dan preferred the new flavor and turned the small experiment into a permanent change to their recipe.[76] It tasted better coming out of the still, and it tasted better after barrel aging. Dan now says of his Kentucky mentors: "They were wrong."

This unexpected truckload of the wrong corn turned out to be a happy accident for Dan. Had Dan followed his instinct to send the white corn back, would he have won fewer awards, or none at all, by sticking with the yellow corn? He might have never realized the mistake of *not* experimenting with the white corn. This might prompt us to ask, "What mistakes have I made that I'm blissfully unaware of?"

TEST AND ITERATE LIKE WASHINGTON HEALTH SYSTEM

Brook Ward, President and CEO of Washington Health System, reminds people that, when they try new things, they are "likely to fail, and that's OK, because it helps us get better." The possibility of failure starts with Brook admitting his ideas don't always work out. But even imperfect ideas can be the foundation for iterations that lead to excellence if you have the right culture.[77]

We might agree that testing and learning from an idea isn't a failure. But how many leaders demand perfection and certainty when their organization tries something new? At WHS, Brook has reacted to mistakes by telling people, "That didn't work, and that's wonderful," even if that surprises some employees. He wouldn't react to a fatal medication error that way. He's responding constructively to mistakes made in attempts to create innovative processes and systems for better care.

Unlike most hospitals, WHS has never hired a traveler nurse in its long history (including during Covid times). "Travelers" are contractors hired through a firm at a cost that's far higher to the hospital while also providing higher pay to the nurse.

While traveler nurses are highly skilled and capable, bringing "strangers" into a care team creates the risk of quality problems and patient harm, simply because they know how to be nurses but don't know how to be nurses at WHS. For a culture to be consistent, new employees and leaders need to be inculcated in the expectations of how the organization works and the mindsets around experimenting and solving problems.

Brook has two main objectives for using full-time staff instead of traveler nurses: improving patient safety and providing excellent care at a lower cost. If WHS left schedule slots unfilled by simply refusing to hire travelers, they would spend less on payroll, but patient care would suffer, which is unacceptable to Brook.

WHS created an alternative way to ensure that all shifts are covered appropriately by incentivizing full-time WHS nurses to pick them up. In describing these innovation efforts, Brook uses the word "iterate" quite often. They didn't have the perfect solution at the beginning. When we spoke in November 2022, this internal shift-coverage system was on the "fourth or fifth" iteration.

If win/win solutions are good, the incentive system for WHS-employed nurses to take on extra shifts is win/win/win:

- Lower cost for the system

- Higher pay for the nurses (they earn almost as much as being a traveler without having to quit, lose their seniority, and be on the road constantly)

- Better outcomes for patients (safety, quality of care, and patient-experience scores).

How do they iterate and improve? Hospital leaders frequently meet with nurses to learn what's working and not working. They've adjusted the system to address concerns about burnout or fatigue. If unaddressed, burnout leads to more nurses getting fatigued or quitting, increasing the risk of mistakes and harm.

80% CAN BE GOOD ENOUGH

Experimenting with a new approach means that we know it will be imperfect, and that's OK. We need to start our small test of change with a reasonably solid hypothesis that things will work well or well enough. But we could be wrong.

An "80% solution" can often be good enough to start moving forward with, realizing you will iterate and improve in ways that get closer to 100% effectiveness. The ability to learn from mistakes, iterate, and improve is certainly not an excuse to test wild ideas that aren't thought out.

WHS is running what they describe as "a pilot" of another new system, a team-based nursing approach in a single unit, which Brook describes as their inpatient "innovation unit." An innovation unit must have team members who are willing to: learn, "take pride in developing new ways," and "thrive on change" (being open to testing ideas).

"We've found this concept not only provides a safe place specifically designed to test ideas, many of which don't work, but it also changes the organization's entire culture. People are testing ideas everywhere [within WHS] because team members understand that trying to improve is expected and that mistakes don't result in blame or punishment."

A small test of change mitigates the risk that the initial design is lacking or imperfect. We're more likely to feel safe learning from early mistakes when done on a smaller scale, where it's easier to admit a small mistake. Based on the initial 12-week experiment, WHS will decide if it should continue (and results in the first six weeks were encouraging) and whether it will spread that model to other units (continuing to iterate and improve along the way). WHS is also using the PDSA (Plan, Do, Study, Adjust) approach throughout the pilot to ensure iteration continues, improving the pilot idea as the team learns.

Thinking that we will implement an improvement and being certain it will work is a very different mindset from testing a hypothesis on a small scale before scaling it more broadly. Toyota directly influenced and mentored Brook and the WHS team, realizing the hospital could learn and adapt the culture and leadership style of a company that's very different from theirs.

ITERATE YOUR UNDERSTANDING TO REPLACE ASSUMPTIONS WITH CLARITY

Melissa Perri is the founder and CEO of Product Institute, a senior lecturer at Harvard Business School, and the author of *Escaping the Build Trap*.

As a product manager (employee #35) at a startup, she wrote a 30-page specifications document telling developers what to build. Three weeks later, when the software was ready for testing, Melissa discovered it didn't meet her needs. "It was nothing that I specified."[78]

What happened? The startup used a common software-development process called "waterfall," so named because the work flows in only one direction. It is a decidedly non-iterative process, which increases the risk of problems.

The developers didn't like reading long documents. Even if they did, these documents were never perfectly written or perfectly understood. Instead of throwing documents and software across the proverbial wall to each other, we can collaborate better in more interactive and iterative ways. In the waterfall method, bad assumptions lead to mistakes. The product manager might make flawed assumptions about what the users actually want. She could be wrong. The developers might make incorrect assumptions about the meaning and intent of the specs. They could be wrong.

After "three months of butting heads," the developers suggested using a newer methodology called "Agile," an iterative approach to building software rooted in the principles of the Toyota Production System and Lean Management. Their overall effectiveness was high; by spending more time *talking about* the work, they gained more clarity and prevented the need to rework the code than by trying to fix problems more quickly. Agile also improved the workplace environment, as everyone started to enjoy working with each other, Melissa recalls.

Later, Melissa realized she had made another mistake. They were using the wrong measures to gauge success for one of the new products they had built using the Agile approach. On the first day, user numbers were high but immediately after started falling to the point where "nobody was using it a month later." This frustrated Melissa.

What happened? Potential users had told her they *wanted* a product with a certain set of features. Why weren't users coming back? Melissa learned, "In hindsight, none of [what they created] was necessary."

No matter how fast and effective your software-development efforts are, spending three months building unnecessary software is an expensive mistake. We don't want to do the wrong things more effectively.

Melissa was inspired to learn newly developed "Lean Startup" ideas from Eric Ries and Steve Blank. For example, instead of merely asking "What *can* we build?" she started taking experimentation and iteration further upstream. This meant first asking and validating assumptions around the question, "What *should* we build?"

We can test hypotheses about a startup in easy, inexpensive ways before investing the time and money required to build anything significant. When using traditional surveys or market research, we might believe people who *say* they would pay for something, only to find out later that they'd made a bad prediction about following through on that intent.

Instead, startups can more effectively test their assumptions in the market, by, for example, quickly building a simple "landing page" that describes the problem our startup is trying to solve and a little bit about our hypothesis about how the product or services will help. If nobody finds the page through an internet search (or paid ads), it's possible nobody cares about the problem enough to search for it—or the language we're using is missing the mark.

If a person *does* find that landing page, we can ask if they're willing to share their email address to receive updates about our startup in exchange. That indicates they are a possible customer, but that might be wrong. It's better, albeit more expensive, to see how many people will actually enter their credit-card number to buy an initial, limited version of a product or service that Ries dubbed a "Minimum Viable Product."

We might learn we need to adjust (or "pivot" in Lean Startup speak) our solution or company based on what we learn. Instead of *knowing* the product or startup will succeed, we can test that idea to learn and iterate as needed. If we're willing to admit mistakes and adjust, being wrong early on can help us eventually get things right. A "Lean Startup" learns as quickly and inexpensively as it can. It's not about being cheap or frugal as the primary objective. The goal is finding "validated learning," as Ries calls it, as quickly and efficiently as possible.

Innovative entrepreneurs (or anybody with a small idea to improve our existing work) must be confident enough to think they have a good idea worth sharing. Again, being confidently humble means believing we *might* have a good idea and feeling strongly enough to speak up in a safe environment. But we could be wrong. We all make mistakes; what matters is learning from them.

EMBRACE YOUR INNOVATION MISTAKES

We all make mistakes, and that's especially true when we are trying to innovate.

Entrepreneur Kurt Wilkin says, "If you don't make mistakes, you're not trying, and you're not growing. If there's anything I could impart to my team, it's to try to make a mistake, learn from it, and move on. If you don't make mistakes, you're not entrepreneurial enough—you're too safe. And if you don't learn from your mistakes, then we've got a bigger problem."

He concludes, "The more I embrace my mistakes, the more authentic I become to myself and to others," adding, "I invest in people who are humble enough to recognize their mistakes and be a learner. I want to be around people who are willing to make mistakes and then also accept that they do make mistakes."

Leaders like Kurt and others we've learned from so far can cultivate a culture of learning and innovation. Being able to learn from mistakes and helping others do the same is a key to success. Next, we'll learn from organizations that have cultivated a winning culture for a few years, a decade, and almost a century. Much as the flow of mistakes never stops, our efforts to cultivate a garden, or a culture, must be never-ending.

CHAPTER EIGHT

CULTIVATE FOREVER

"There are no gardening mistakes, only experiments."

—JANET KILBURN-PHILLIPS

Owner and head distiller David Meier started Glenns Creek Distilling in 2014. The place feels like a classic garage-based startup, as his primary operations are all housed in what used to be the bottling building for the defunct Old Crow Distillery. Having grown tired of traveling the globe as a consultant for fifteen years, David wanted to start making things again. Being in Kentucky, what came to mind was Bourbon.

David had been inspired by what he learned in previous manufacturing roles, and Glenns Creek was an opportunity for him to start cultivating a culture of problem-solving and learning from mistakes from the beginning. He says, "When I consider whether our culture matches my intent, I only have to consider the people who have full-time jobs elsewhere but come out on weekends to help. They are given the latitude to work on things that help the company and bring them enjoyment."

David says, "Our culture is simple. It's centered around the idea of *kaizen*, the Japanese word for *continuous improvement*." He can't help but transplant the five foundational Toyota principles—challenge, kaizen, go and see, respect, and teamwork.[79] In that spirit, Glenns Creek builds their own custom production equipment, develops their products and recipes, and creates a positive visitor experience. "We improve things using our ideas and creativity." If anybody sees something that can be improved, they can take initiative to test and evaluate their ideas.

David would tell new hires, "You can't make a mistake that hasn't been made here already." He later saw this guidance as flawed since new opportunities for mistakes get created every time the distillery does something new.

In early 2023, Glenns Creek received a huge award for a small company. Their best-selling release, OCD #5 Bourbon, was named the U.S. Micro Whisky of the Year in *Jim Murray's Whisky Bible 2023 North American Edition*. You might recall that Garrison Brothers, mentioned earlier, received the same award in five of the previous seven years. It makes me wonder if the apparent connection between a culture of learning from mistakes and award-winning Bourbon is a matter of correlation or causation.

As a startup, the soil was fertile and ready. But where did David get the seedlings for the Glenns Creek culture? From his decade spent working at the Toyota plant in nearby Georgetown, Kentucky. Unlike companies that try to keep their methods in-house by locking departing employees into non-disclosure agreements, Toyota actively encourages them to share and spread their knowledge to other companies and their communities, as David continues doing today.

TURNING A MISTAKE INTO AN EXPERIMENT

People at companies with an emphasis on learning are more likely to turn mistakes into something positive. One day, the distillery ran out of rye, an essential grain in their whiskey recipes. David would normally ask, "What happened? And why? How can we prevent that from happening again?" In this case, David admits he forgot to order the rye. He tweaked his process a few ways so that he wouldn't repeat that mistake.

Beyond that reactive problem-solving, one of his employees, John, looked for a positive outcome by asking, "What would happen if we made a 100% corn Bourbon?" Not surprisingly, David said, "I don't know" (a healthy habit for a leader) and suggested a small experiment to see (and taste) the result.

If this experiment didn't produce a whiskey worth selling, they would have learned something useful. They would have done so quickly and at a relatively low cost (the raw materials and energy costs). They cooked the "mash," made of ground corn and water, fermented it into a beer-like liquid, and fired up the still. The clear liquid that flowed from the still seemed promising, so it was time for phase two of the experiment. The worst-case scenario would be that the additional cost of learning was a barrel (roughly $1300) and the space required to age it.

After aging the experiment for two years, David loved the unique flavor and was excited to release it as "A-MAIZE-ING

C.O.B. Bourbon" (Corn Only Bourbon), generating revenue on top of learning. He was happy to have produced one of the few 100% corn Bourbons available on the market. David now has better information that he can use to determine if he will distill and age more.

TOYOTA TRANSPLANTED SEEDLINGS TO THE U.S.

In 1987, David was hired by the Toyota Motor Manufacturing Kentucky (TMMK) plant in Georgetown, Kentucky. In between leaving Toyota and founding Glenns Creek, he traveled the world as a consultant to teach others the methods and mindsets he'd learned at Toyota.

As Toyota's first full factory built from the ground up in the United States, TMMK was an expensive endeavor. Toyota first transplanted seedlings to the NUMMI joint venture with GM in California. This relatively inexpensive test of change, having started production in late 1984, demonstrated that Toyota's management system and leadership style could work outside of Japan.

Following that experiment, the TMMK plant was established in 1986 and started production two years later. Part of Toyota's intentional cross-pollination included sending some NUMMI employees to help the new plant get up and running. Thankfully, the seedlings continued growing well in the U.S. and around the world as Toyota learned and improved through repeated Plan-Do-Study-Adjust cycles.

You know an organizational culture is consistent when stories exhibiting the same habits and behaviors can be found in a company across continents and decades. GM had a pervasively negative culture of blaming and screaming, at least in the 1980s and '90s. By the mid-'90s, GM was actively working to emulate the Toyota culture, even if that's easier said than done—especially when the soil was so parched and infertile, if not toxic.

In *Toyota Culture*, Jeff Liker and Mike Hoseus describe environments where people feel safe pointing out problems, including mistakes. "If problems are hidden," they write, "the entire system of continuous improvement stops functioning." They cite an internal publication ("Toyota Way 2001") that promotes organizational learning:

> *"We view errors as opportunities for learning. Rather than blaming individuals, the organization takes corrective actions and distributes knowledge about each experience broadly."*

Toyota stories demonstrate a consistent pattern that can't be a coincidence. Isao Yoshino's story about the paint machine revealed a strong culture of learning from mistakes in 1966. A few decades later, in Japan, Mike Hoseus was applauded for admitting that he scratched a car. You might remember both stories from Chapter Five.

While such a culture seems deeply ingrained, every company must guard against backsliding away from established norms and behaviors. In early 2023, outgoing CEO Akio Toyoda told a group of employees that "young people should be given opportunities to make mistakes and learn from them."[80] Words matter—actions, even more.

David Meier, in late-1980s Kentucky, discovered the consistency of the culture through that time. At age 27, he became a supervisor (called a "group leader" at Toyota). In that role, David managed a group of hourly workers consisting of frontline team members and team leaders who each supported a small group of team members.[81]

Unlike Yoshino, David joined Toyota after working at other companies, which taught him mindsets and habits he had to unlearn. David said, "One of the things I found frustrating [in previous jobs] and which kind of made me angry, was that, when my people would make mistakes, it felt like the blame came down on me [as a leader]."

In comparison, he discovered that "Toyota teaches that the leader's responsibility is to develop and create processes and systems that allow people to do their best work." This culture doesn't just appear; senior leaders and their followers must actively nurture it.

David found habits hard to break. For example, he had come to believe that a person was "stupid" if they made a mistake and to assume they didn't know the correct way to do things. He recalls, "It took me a couple of years to clear my brain of the impulse to blame the worker."

It took many years for David to fully adopt the Toyota approach, which included shifting from blaming workers when they struggled to asking "Why are they struggling?" They weren't looking for the answer to "What's wrong with the employee?" If a team member misunderstood work instructions, David came to recognize it was *his* problem because he was responsible for the work and results, just as it was for Yoshino's managers 20 years earlier.

Cultivate Forever

Like many other high-performing companies, Toyota leaders assume people are intrinsically motivated to do high-quality work. Nobody comes to work looking to make mistakes. As David learned, "You have to understand that, when people make mistakes, it's not intentional." By definition, that is true. In general, I cringe when I hear the phrase "unintended mistake," since that phrase is redundant.

PUTTING DAVID'S NEW UNDERSTANDING TO THE TEST

Five years into his Toyota career, David led a department that molded parts called "bumper cores" that became part of the bumper assembly. One day, at the end of a molding cycle, David's team opened a molding machine to find crumbly powder inside instead of a properly formed part. What happened? Was this new problem the result of a new production mistake?

W. Edwards Deming, the famed American quality guru, taught Toyota, "A bad system will beat a good person every time." Instead of blaming a person, Toyota leaders look for the root cause and other contributing factors, pointing them to improve processes, instead of blaming (and possibly replacing) people. Mistakes cannot be prevented by proactively firing all of the mistake-prone people—because that's all of us. We'll all make mistakes in a bad system.

A team of experienced problem-solvers, including David, concluded the automated machine wasn't pulling the correct material. Or the machine wasn't mixing it properly. Or both. They were wrong. They had assumed that a machine malfunction was causing the problem and jumped to countermeasures, draining the machine and filling it manually. Six or seven hours later, the crumbly powder problem remained.

Toyota suffered costs of at least $8.3 million from the bumpers that were never available for vehicle production. And while that was probably a low estimate, he recalls that "No one was yelling or screaming about the cost of the problem."

Later, the team recognized their problem-solving mistake. They had forgotten to take what David says should always be the first step in Toyota's problem-solving method: verifying how the work was supposed to be done. Remember Yoshino's story from Chapter Five? Yoshino's managers asked him to show them the process by which he poured the cans into the tank. They verified the standard.

When the Kentucky team finally did this, they discovered that a materials mixup was causing the problem. Just like Yoshino's story from decades earlier in Japan, somebody had put an incorrect chemical into the molding machine: a solvent instead of a catalyst.

At Toyota, problem-solvers use structured methods, including what is popularly described as the "Five Whys" process. What matters is asking "Why?" as many times as necessary to find a root cause or causes. It might require five, or fewer, or more.

Why were the bumper cores not forming properly? A solvent had been loaded instead of a catalyst. Why? An unneeded solvent was in the area. Why? It had been delivered there. Why? Instead of punishing a person, they would keep asking "Why?" until they could identify and test countermeasures intended to prevent this problem from recurring.

When verifying the standard, David also learned that the formal work instructions did not have the machine operator verify the chemicals before loading them. When the team discovered this, they were able to update these job instructions easily. To be fair to the people who wrote them, it's understandable why they wouldn't have included a step intended to detect a problem that hadn't happened before. Even if the delivery problem would never be repeated, that short verification step prevented some major risks.

Toyota also noticed that the drum containing the wrong material was the same color and size as the one they normally used, containing the catalyst. Knowing that human inspection (visually verifying the chemical) would never be 100% reliable (because we are all human and make mistakes), Toyota asked the manufacturer to change the color of the correct chemical's drum, so that it was different from the one that was mistakenly used—an example of mistake-proofing.

Having addressed the production mistake with multiple countermeasures, they could also dig into the problem-solving mistake. Had the team solved that problem more quickly, they would have reduced or prevented the multi-million-dollar loss. Digging into their problem-solving process, they asked why a team of twenty-five people had walked past that incorrect drum for hours without thinking to stop and check it. Then again, why would they even think to do so if the wrong chemical had never been delivered before?

Looking back, David believes "groupthink" had prevented anybody from asking if they should double-check the materials being used. One key lesson he learned was to have somebody stay back to be an observer (and a coach) of the problem-solving efforts. He concludes, "I am convinced the issue was so far outside anything ever encountered that everyone panicked. Even the best, most skilled problem-solvers make mistakes."

As with Yoshino's story, leaders focused on learning and improving their processes. David didn't feel blamed for either of the mistakes related to the chemical or the problem-solving. He remembers how TMMK president Fujio Cho, who later became Toyota's chairman, always asked "What did we learn today?" as he did the day of David's story.

SHARE THE BOUNTY OF YOUR MISTAKES

When the organization learns from a mistake and improves processes, it can share the story and the improvements with other teams who do similar work, helping them proactively eliminate opportunities to make exactly the same mistake. On one level, any other Toyota facility that's molding bumper cores would benefit from that. But what if the sharing extended to any molding operation making any part? Or to any process where chemicals are being added to a machine, including paint shops?

Ideally, Toyota would have shared all of the lessons from Yoshino's 1960s story with all facilities and implemented mistake-proofing measures. This would have effectively eliminated the opportunity for David's story. How likely is it for a similar mixup to happen at a Toyota facility today? Or in the future, as new vehicle technologies and new production processes are invented?

Cultivate Forever

How can our organizations (or entire industries) propagate lessons learned, so that everybody doesn't have to learn, on their own, from making that same mistake? Learning from our own mistakes is great, but learning from the mistakes of others is even better.

SPREADING THE CULTURE WITHIN TOYOTA

In writing about Toyota's culture, there might be times when it's helpful (or more accurate) to describe its manufacturing culture. Since the origin of the Toyota Production System was in, well, production, we couldn't assume that the same mindsets would automatically appear all throughout various company functions. Instead of relying on the wind to spread seeds naturally, leaders can do so intentionally.

In 1998, Matthew E. May started working for Toyota's newly opened corporate-education center in California. During his eight years there, he worked to help spread the Toyota Production System (and culture) into knowledge-work functions.[82]

He learned how Toyota manufacturing has specific improvement mindsets and methodologies. Instead of simply accepting a single, definitive-sounding solution to a problem, managers ask, "What other countermeasures did you consider?" They also tend not to use the word "solution" because problems are rarely fully "solved" in the real world.[83] In Toyota plants, a countermeasure is a "temporary response to specific problems that will serve until a better approach is found or conditions change."[84]

Instead of assuming their ideas are good, Toyota factory personnel have a strong habit of conducting small experiments, testing countermeasures to learn if they are ineffective, very effective, or somewhere in between. Matt says an idea would be tested on a small scale before going department-wide, nationwide, or company-wide. After a successful small-scale test, Matt learned to ask, "What would have to be true for this to be good on a broader scale?" instead of assuming that spreading an improvement would be effective and beneficial.

Matt found there was, generally, more creativity on the Toyota shop floors than could be found in the so-called "carpet land" office areas. Why? It was a function of culture and leadership behaviors. He recalls, "There was a fear of failure on the knowledge side of the business." In particular, "The 'fail fast and learn' mentality was not there." An experimental mindset, or a culture of learning from mistakes, is the result of what leaders say and, more importantly, what they do as they cultivate a culture of learning from mistakes—and what they do to spread it (or to test the idea of spreading it on a small scale).

In recent years, Toyota has embraced experimental methodologies in IT and technology areas, including Agile software development. Eric Ries says what he learned about TPS from books is the basis for his "Lean Startup" methodologies. Things came full circle in about 2012, when a Toyota team asked for Eric's help in learning and applying Lean Startup concepts to rapidly develop, test, and iterate a new vehicle navigation and entertainment system, shifting away from the old "waterfall" method, mentioned in Chapter Seven.[85]

Cultivate Forever

TRANSPLANTING TOYOTA'S SEEDS
INTO AN ACQUIRED COMPANY

Toyota Motor Corporation's culture of learning from mistakes has incredibly deep and hardy roots. Even so, Toyota must teach the culture to every new employee and at every new site and business unit. The cultivation never stops.

In 2000, Toyota Industries acquired The Raymond Corporation, a manufacturer of material-handling equipment. Before joining Raymond in 2018, Keith Ingels worked for a Toyota Material Handling equipment dealership for more than a decade, with a stop at another company in between.

Keith is the Raymond Lean Management (RLM) manager of Solutions and Support Centers, with RLM being based on the Toyota Production System. Keith prefers the RLM name, since the company has its own identity, history, and culture. Raymond faced the challenge of improving an existing culture, not for the sake of emulating Toyota, but to become more successful in its business. Today, Raymond says they have studied and implemented TPS throughout its organization, but they consider RLM to be a one-of-a-kind lean-management system.[86]

Raymond benefits from mistakes Keith has made in his past, including his favorite-mistake story about initially misunderstanding the purpose of "5S," a well-known Toyota method. As Keith learned, "5S is not housekeeping. It starts as housekeeping, but it's really about workplace readiness."[87] Keith made the common mistake of copying a tool without fully understanding its purpose. But he learned and adjusted, and now helps others avoid making that mistake.

Keith says cultivating the culture is a lot of work, but worth it. Raymond leaders teach that mistakes are not just OK but can have positive outcomes, even referring to them as "treasures," as part of an unlearning that must occur. Since, as Keith emphasizes, we cannot fix a problem that we cannot find, leaders work to create conditions where people feel safe to speak up—the first step in problem-solving.

A LITTLE STRUGGLE CAN PRODUCE BETTER RESULTS

At Raymond, Keith noticed that another piece of the culture is allowing people to learn from mistakes. One day, Keith observed an RLM trainer giving students the answer to a question he had posed. Keith stopped the trainer and suggested he not give the answer.

The trainer said, "They weren't getting it."

"Mistakes are great teachers," Keith says. If we get something right the first time, "I might have gotten lucky, and the learning wouldn't necessarily stick." But if they do something less than perfectly, they will remember what they've learned from that.

Even though it might seem efficient to help a student do it right the first time, Keith notes if the struggle helps the student, then it is valuable. If this means that problem-solving and improvement happen more slowly, we must accept that the deeper learning that occurs delivers far more long-term benefits than costs to the organization.

Thinking back to David Meier's problem-solving challenges in the molding department, we might wonder if a more-senior person would have provided what they believed to be the right answer, such as, "You're adding the wrong chemical."

Would they have given the answer, leading to a faster resolution (and reducing that multi-million-dollar loss)? Or would they let the team learn more through their struggle? Organizations might consider a tradeoff between short-term costs and possible long-term benefits, but Toyota is known for making decisions based on the long term, even at the expense of the short term.[88]

Raymond also guards against our common human tendency to rush problem-solving and improvement work, especially when the situation is urgent (as we saw in David's Toyota story). Jumping quickly to an assumed cause greatly slowed their problem-solving.

Keith teaches that it's counterintuitive that slowing down can speed up our problem-solving. He used a famous expression that's attributed to many, including Charles Kettering, GM's former head of research and holder of nearly 200 patents: "A problem well-defined is a problem half solved."

Spending more time on the "Plan" stage of the Plan-Do-Study-Adjust cycle helps us avoid getting sidetracked. We're more likely to understand the real causes of a problem and start testing countermeasures that are more likely to work. They are more likely to be sustained because we've more deeply engaged all the right people in the process.

We don't need to be a massive company like Toyota to cultivate a culture of learning from mistakes. We can see it at small companies like the Garrison Brothers and Glenns Creek distilleries, and software companies like KaiNexus.

HOW A DOCTOR CULTIVATES THE CULTURE
AT A SOFTWARE COMPANY

You don't install or upgrade culture like a piece of software, nor do you program it precisely with zeros and ones. Since KaiNexus developed a web-based platform that organizations use to manage improvement work, co-founders Greg Jacobson, MD (CEO), and Matt Paliulis (COO) realized from the beginning that the company should emulate the continuous-improvement culture of its customers.

The organizational soil was fertile from the beginning, so KaiNexus leaders planted seeds by admitting their mistakes, among other vulnerable acts.[89] "I don't think you create a culture. It's the result of the way you act," says Greg, so leaders nurture the culture by continually rewarding those who speak up about mistakes, concerns, or improvement ideas.

In the early years of the company, Greg doesn't remember talking directly with the team about avoiding blame and learning from mistakes. It was easier for the co-founders to influence the culture because they were interacting with everybody every day. They set the tone for others by choosing improvement over punishment, and I don't remember them ever reacting angrily to a mistake or setback.

As the company grew beyond 15 employees, Greg says, "It wasn't until 2018 or '19 that we realized we had a culture." At that point, the culture was in good shape, but Greg and the leadership team decided to be intentional about their cultivation so it could continue thriving, otherwise, the culture "could get out of hand," Greg says.

The team identified the guiding values and traits that contributed to individual and organizational success. At KaiNexus, these lists are shared and discussed during the new-employee-onboarding process, and it's regularly reviewed and discussed in company meetings.

The values and partial description:

- We are a team ("Help others reach their full potential")

- Trust and be trustworthy ("People achieve their maximum potential in high-trust environments")

- Show empathy ("Put yourself in the shoes of others")

- Serve customers first

The fifth value says, "Be Kind: Be kind to one another, be kind to our customers, be kind to others—this includes being accepting and inclusive of other cultures, beliefs, and all peoples."

As KaiNexus is now much more intentional about cultivating its culture, Greg recognizes the importance of psychological safety and prompts others to discuss it more directly; he models behaviors that help others feel safe speaking up. "People in safe cultures don't hide mistakes," he says.

RE-ANALYZING THE SOIL: THE CURRENT STATE OF PSYCHOLOGICAL SAFETY

Again, Timothy R. Clark defines psychological safety as "a culture of rewarded vulnerability," where people feel safe to be themselves, to learn and contribute, and feel safe to challenge the status quo. Leaders might feel like they have created a generally safe environment but sometimes make the mistake of assuming that others will feel safe, since they do, or they overestimate the level of safety felt by others.

Leaders can assess the current state of an organization's culture. Ideally, we could have direct conversations with employees at all levels. But it's hard to talk honestly about a lack of psychological safety when a team doesn't feel safe speaking with candor. Don't make the mistake of asking leading questions where the only apparent safe answer is "Yes," such as, "Do you feel safe to speak up?"

In late 2022, KaiNexus invited every employee to complete an anonymous survey created by Clark's organization, LeaderFactor. The survey asked people to state their level of agreement with twelve statements, including "I am allowed to learn from my mistakes."

Every KaiNexian responded with a seven or higher (out of ten), and 84% answered nine or ten. On that statement, KaiNexus ranked in the 80th percentile of all teams who had been surveyed by LeaderFactor worldwide. Overall, KaiNexus ranked in the 78th percentile across all twelve questions, meaning there is a generally high level of psychological safety overall, across all four stages. Stating that doesn't mean every KaiNexian feels equally safe in every situation. Some individuals might feel less safe because of being new to the company, experiences at previous companies, or other factors.

KaiNexus didn't use the survey because we thought a safety problem existed. The leadership team and I wanted to ensure that the company had a reasonably high psychological-safety level. Even with that assumption, we looked for opportunities to improve and strengthen the culture, learning from responses to questions, including, "What is one thing that prevents you from feeling safe to challenge the status quo of your team?"

Conducting short training sessions about psychological safety and sharing the survey results have sparked ongoing discussions among leaders and teams. This helps KaiNexus leaders realize (and remember) they cannot mandate psychological safety. They must create conditions in which people can decide they feel safe.

The survey prompted KaiNexus to discuss ways we help people feel more included, accepted, and respected (Stage One, inclusion safety, in Clark's psychological-safety framework). They discuss how to help KaiNexians feel safer to ask questions or to say, "I don't know." (Stage Two, learner safety). Are people allowed to do their jobs with the appropriate level of guidance and autonomy (Stage Three, contributor safety)? Innovation and peak performance happen when people feel safe challenging the status quo (Stage Four, challenger safety).

The point, of course, isn't higher survey scores. What matters is being better at retaining talent, innovating, and serving customers, which KaiNexus expects to drive continued growth and better performance.

ADMIT MISTAKES, AND ASK, "WHAT CAN WE LEARN?"

"I made mistakes."

At least two leaders at KaiNexus made that simple declarative statement during the company's all-hands meeting for about thirty-five employees in July 2022. They didn't use the weaselly passive language of "Mistakes were made."

During these biannual meetings, each KaiNexian shares highlights from the past six months, including "What went well?" That's easy to do. Most companies love sharing success stories.

Each employee also shares things that didn't go well, discussing:

- What can we improve?

- What did we learn?

Chief revenue officer Jeff Roussel told the team, "I made a mistake," telling the story of the first hiring mistake he made in his eight years with the company. Instead of making excuses or deflecting responsibility, Jeff owned his actions and explained how he didn't take the advice of another senior leader, Maggie Millard, who expressed concerns about the candidate. At least she felt safe to disagree.

It quickly became apparent that the new salesperson didn't share some of the core beliefs and mindsets that generally help somebody succeed at KaiNexus. Other KaiNexians raised concerns to senior leaders about the new person.

After coaching the salesperson, it became clear the only resolution to the hiring mistake was to let them go. Jeff and the leadership team didn't ask, "What was wrong with that person?" Instead, they reflected on the hiring process, trying to understand what had gone wrong and, more importantly, what they could do differently going forward.

Jeff was kind to himself, but the leadership focused on making constructive changes. KaiNexus now allows any leadership-team member to veto a potential new hire. They have a new hypothesis to test. Is that veto option a mistake that solves some problems while creating others? Only time will tell, but KaiNexus will react, learn, and adjust accordingly.

After the company meeting, as a way to continue emphasizing these crucial elements of the culture, Jeff shared with the team: "So many of you showed trust by being vulnerable during your presentations and by talking openly about the good and the bad things happening at KaiNexus. And the honest-but-fair questions everyone asked demonstrated the trustworthy way we act toward one another."

Greg and Matt lead regular "retrospectives" with the development team after each new release of the KaiNexus software platform. The team focuses not just on quality software as an outcome; they also improve the processes that bring software updates to customers.

"We're going to focus on the process to see if we can eliminate mistakes" that occurred in the past or proactively work to prevent new mistakes that might happen in the future. "I like to think we do a good job of it," says Greg.

START CULTIVATING, AND PLAN TO KEEP IT GOING

In the introduction, I compared the high-level garden-cultivating process to what's required to initiate, grow, and sustain a workplace culture. The word "cultivate" suggests leaders must continually nourish the culture by providing proper amounts of food, water, and sunlight. We can't "implement" a culture of learning from mistakes any more than we can "install" psychological safety through a quick, one-off initiative.

Cultivation is a process with many steps. It starts with intent. But then we have to do the work—the right work, the right way. After ensuring the soil is ready, leaders can plant the seeds. As the culture begins to germinate, others will participate. And it will get stronger as long as we can keep away those who might destroy our culture—pests and pestilence.

DECLARE YOUR INTENT

Much like deciding where to plant a garden, cultivating our culture starts with declaring our intent. Much as we might think about what vegetables we'd like to eat from our garden, the founder or CEO of an organization might think through the behaviors they'd like to see sprouting and thriving. These might include:

- Modeling and rewarding vulnerable acts to strengthen feelings of psychological safety

- Admitting mistakes

- Saying, "I could be wrong"

- Using mistake-proofing methods instead of telling people to be more careful

- Testing hypotheses and assumptions instead of implementing solutions

- Replacing punishment with learning and improvement to prevent future mistakes

- Using small tests of change to prevent huge mistakes

Before declaring this intent, leaders should start by being kind to themselves when they make mistakes, as discussed in Chapter Two.

Hopefully, this book will result in more executives declaring this intent as their new direction. Others will discover what had been growing organically in their organization like a wild plant that started growing where conditions were right, with a newly declared intent to tend to it, actively shaping their culture instead of letting it evolve.

We shouldn't just throw seeds into the ground without understanding if the conditions are right for those plants to grow. We need to remove obvious barriers like rocks, weeds, or debris, represented by behaviors like yelling, blaming, and punishing after mistakes.

We can measure the perceived level of psychological safety through survey instruments like the one described earlier in this chapter. If we didn't analyze the soil before we started the garden, we might find the need to do so if our plants are struggling, or if we're just trying to take our garden from good to great. If the organizational soil is too acidic, remedial actions might be needed to help build psychological safety before we start asking people to speak up about mistakes.

PLANT THE SEEDS

Once the soil seems ready enough, leaders plant the seeds by going first and leading by example—modeling vulnerable acts. These include admitting mistakes or saying, "I'm not certain this idea is completely right, so let's test it and see what we learn."

When people start testing the waters by doing the same, leaders need to reward those vulnerable acts, starting a reinforcing loop that helps the culture grow.

If you sense (or measure) that your organization does not have a culture of learning from mistakes, the good news is that you can start cultivating it. Ideally, that starts with the CEO and senior leaders. If not, you can start within your part of the organization and hope that your efforts to cherish and learn from mistakes don't get uprooted by an executive who still demands punishment.

CONTINUALLY CARE FOR THE PLANTS

It takes time to cultivate this culture, but it's doable. No garden grows overnight. It takes sustained effort over time to build trust and psychological safety.

It might be a mistake to compare employees to plants, but both need appropriate levels of water, food, and sunshine. The fuel for the culture garden's growth is provided by leaders who react to mistakes in kind and constructive ways, the food and water. The fertilizer of effective problem-solving and improvement methods ensures that reporting mistakes leads to a reduction in mistakes. Transparency is needed in organizations as gardens need sunshine. Organizations that share mistakes and lessons learned will drive more improvement and better performance.

I believe that an organization with a culture of learning from mistakes will be more successful than a competitor that does not. I am looking forward to testing that hypothesis with more organizations. Learning from mistakes allows us to be more innovative. This means not just improving what we do, but also creating new products and services that allow the organization to be more successful long term.

Organizations that learn from mistakes should experience lower turnover than others, since its people will feel more respected. We get a direct financial benefit when we reduce the cost of attrition. Better yet, we'll have longer-tenured employees who are more deeply engaged in the organization and aligned with its success.

We see this culture at companies as wide-ranging as the globally huge Toyota and small-yet-growing KaiNexus. Neither company is perfect, but learning from mistakes is their ideal, and their ongoing and intentional cultivation efforts set a nice example.

Research and experience show leaders how to cultivate this culture: modeling and rewarding vulnerable acts, including admitting we could be wrong and that we make mistakes. Following that guidance, we should expect to make mistakes along this journey. For example, if a CEO has a lousy day and reacts poorly to a mistake, the story might spread across the organization, making others feel less safe, but reflection and an honest apology might mitigate the damage. Inviting others to give candid feedback can help prevent a small mistake from turning into a catastrophic pattern. If the roots of the new culture have become deep and strong, a single leadership mistake is less likely to poison the soil and our garden.

KEEP THE PESTS OUT

Even the hardiest, prettiest garden faces threats, including weather and insects. Even the best organizational cultures cannot grow forever. Unfortunately, slow, steady progress in improving the culture can be demolished when leaders behave badly. Other threats might be more subtle and insidious—even one bad hire might start rotting the plants and poisoning the soil through behaviors that make people feel less psychologically safe. It's best to keep the pests out, through effective interviewing and screening practices. Leaders must be vigilant that their behavior doesn't slip and that they aren't ignorant (or tolerant) of bad behaviors that appear, such as leaders reacting unkindly, "naming, blaming, and shaming," or choosing punishment over learning.

START CULTIVATING AND EXPERIMENTING

Hopefully, the stories and examples in this book will help you feel more confident in starting or continuing your cultural cultivation. You might be starting from scratch, like Glenns Creek or KaiNexus. Or, you might be in the midst of a culture-change effort like the Raymond Corporation.

Instead of looking for a perfect roadmap, think more like a GPS guidance system. If you know your starting point (including the baseline level of psychological safety) and your destination (stating your intent to have a thriving culture of learning from mistakes), a traditional map could help. But maps quickly get outdated. When we run into a massive traffic jam, it's easier to choose the best alternative route with GPS than even the most up-to-date map.

Among advocates of the Lean Startup methodology, the traditional five-year business plan is considered as outdated as a thick paper map book for a city. Think like an experimentalist, not a planner. The proven model of Plan-Do-Study-Adjust remains helpful.

Beyond declaring your intent and destination, state your assumptions and hypothesis. What must be true for your culture to survive and thrive? What is your hypothesis about the benefits and expected outcomes you expect to see from this work?

Use small tests of change when possible, and have the leader go first. Close the loop by checking your assumptions. Did they pan out, or have you found opportunities for learning and adjusting? Do your actual outcomes match your expectations? If not, keep asking "Why?" and try countermeasures that you predict will continue closing your culture gap—and your performance gaps.

Expect to make mistakes. And remind yourself that's okay. Maybe you'll have one to discuss in an episode of *My Favorite Mistake*. We're all human, even founders and CEOs. Admit your mistakes, reflect, learn, adjust, and keep moving forward—better.

AFTERWORD

I'd like to share a few reflections on a few things I've learned in the process of hosting *My Favorite Mistake* and writing this book. I hope the lessons connect to your work, whether that's writing a book or improving and innovating in other endeavors and settings.

TAKING ON NEW CHALLENGES AND LEARNING FROM MISTAKES

I'm glad I took on a new challenge, the podcast, that was outside of my usual professional boundaries. Investing time in the podcast certainly hasn't been a mistake. I have made so many mistakes along the way, more than could be shared in this book, and I've worked to learn and adjust—not making the same mistake more than once (okay, maybe twice). When my guests made mistakes, I hope I reacted kindly and constructively. Beyond just giving (or accepting) an apology, I've focused on improving my process in ways that would prevent mistakes from being repeated.

I hope this book helps you take on new challenges with a mindset of expecting mistakes and taking steps to minimize the risk of huge mistakes or embarrassment. And hopefully, more people will be willing and able to share their mistakes. What's your favorite mistake? Your most recent? What's the last mistake that you've called out, to yourself or others? Can you find an opportunity to call one out today?

REMEMBERING TO BE POSITIVE ABOUT MISTAKES

My guests and their stories provide comfort to me as a mistake-maker, and I hope they have the same effect on you. The strength, resilience, and kindness demonstrated by my guests served as continual inspiration for me during some turbulent and stressful times.

I already knew we all make mistakes. This experience has turned my suspicion that we can be better off *because* of our mistakes into a strong belief. I learned there are many leaders who aren't just tolerating mistakes, they are cherishing them as gifts that can drive organizational improvement and personal growth. I hope the book gives you more confidence to pursue this path.

I've learned the difference between "nice" and "kind," and that we can move beyond, saying, "That's okay—it's not your fault" to a kind approach that adds, "Let's work together to prevent this from happening again." I'm still working on it, but this helps me be kinder to myself when it's often easier to be kind toward others and their mistakes. This experience has reinforced that I'm not alone in thinking that the punitive approach isn't a pathway to improvement, let alone perfection.

Afterword

FINDING OR STARTING A BETTER GARDEN FOR GROWTH

Some readers might feel stuck working in an ugly garden that's full of weeds and hazards. If you're in that situation, I hope the book inspires you to seek out workplaces where leaders are cultivating a more constructive culture. When interviewing for a new role or job, I hope more people will ask their prospective managers questions like, "Tell me about a time an employee made a mistake and how you handled it." You can learn a lot about the soil in their garden through such a question. Will it allow you to grow and thrive?

What can you do to create those conditions? I also hope the book inspires entrepreneurs to start cultivating their culture garden from the start. If you don't like the workplace garden you're in now, create an opportunity to start a new one with fresh, fertile soil, focusing not just on the problems you want to solve for potential customers but also on the culture that can help propel you to success.

ITERATE YOUR WAY TO SUCCESS

One of this book's main themes is the broader idea of iterating our way to success, and, indeed, this book has evolved in many ways over a year. I hope it's for the better. I could be wrong. On that note, what's the last time you remember distinguishing between what you *know* to be true versus what you *suspect* to be true? Can you call out moments when you might be wrong, inviting others to challenge you or to test your assumptions together in an open and honest way?

My original concept was to share some collected stories and reflections from my guests. I think taking that approach would have been a mistake. Simply sharing a collection of stories might have been a lost opportunity for me to think and learn more about this topic of learning from mistakes.

When I started writing, the words drew heavily on large sections that weren't anything more than verbatim excerpts from episode transcripts. Thankfully, my book coach, Cathy Fyock, and my developmental editor, Tom Ehrenfeld, both encouraged me to trust and rely more on my voice, thoughts, stories, and reflections. The idea wasn't to turn this into a memoir but to use stories and quotes to illustrate key points that I wanted to make. In my first drafts, my telling of many of these tales was unnecessarily long, and iteration led to more-efficient versions of the stories that served the same purpose.

I initially struggled with how to structure the book, so I took advice from my coach and editor, who each told me just to start writing, with the expectation of figuring it out. It might have been ideal to develop the perfect outline before writing, but that just wasn't happening. Anyway, nobody ever writes a perfect book in their head before typing. Writing and editing are iterative processes, especially when you don't start with a perfectly conceived outline (and I did not). I hope the book helps you in situations where you are stuck, in writing or creating anything new. Focus on progress over perfection. It's usually better to get started and then iterate based on feedback and your own reflections.

Over time, a core message of my book converged with my own activity: I came to trust the process and, above all, developed the mindset of responding constructively and learning. I became more willing to try out new approaches, reflect on the work, and let my garden grow. I cultivated a growth mindset.

At one point, I also realized I was trying to write what started to seem like two books in one—a bit of a self-help book for individuals and a management book—serving neither purpose well. So, I cut a few chapters and set them aside for other possible uses. Instead of feeling bad about the mistake of writing chapters I didn't use, I focused on what I learned in the process. I hope the book helps you focus as much on what you learned from a mistake as on figuring out why it happened.

During the writing process, one of my podcast guests, journalist and author Mike Ulmer, told me, "If you end up publishing the book you thought you were going to write, then something went wrong in the process." What he means is that our thinking inevitably evolves along the way. The writing and editing iterations helped me better understand ideas and state them more clearly and succinctly. In iterations with process improvement or entrepreneurship, I hope that you don't view it as a failure when it makes sense to tweak your original project or business concept. If we're not evolving and not iterating, that means we're not learning.

It's always challenging to take a bunch of interconnected concepts and present them in the linear flow of a book. There might not have been one best way to structure this book. I hope readers are helped by the idea that producing something good enough is better than agonizing over whether another approach would have been better.

The subtitle underwent cycles of iteration, and my cover designer, Don Coon, gave me a huge gift by suggesting the word

"Cultivating" which led to some iteration of the book's contents, especially in Chapters One and Eight. Speaking of the cover, its creation was also a fun, collaborative, and iterative process, evolving from Don's initial pencil-sketch concepts to a dozen iterations on the way to finalizing the chosen design. Instead of testing these decisions in the marketplace, I relied on advice from some trusted advisors, but the final decisions are mine, and any mistakes are also mine.

FROM ITERATION TO COMPLETION

The iteration could have been never-ending. I've passed along the advice I received years ago to other authors: "You're never really finished with a book; at some point, you just decide to stop working on it." As entrepreneurs have taught me, nothing's ever perfect. As my book coach said, it's better to publish an imperfect book than keep trying to perfect a draft forever. I hope this book helps you work on preventing mistakes while realizing nobody is perfect and no organization is mistake-free.

I hope you enjoyed the book and find it useful. I couldn't prevent all writing mistakes, and I couldn't expect my editors and proofreaders to find every mistake. Human inspection, including proofreading, is never 100% effective. But I hope you appreciate our efforts.

I'd love to hear feedback about what you liked, what you learned, and how you'll use this book. I also hope you'd feel safe enough to point out mistakes (large or small). Being the publisher, and with on-demand printing, I can continue to iterate the book after its release, whether that means fixing a typo or correcting a factual error. You can email me at Mark@MarkGraban.com.

I'll close by repeating the mantras on my *My Favorite Mistake* coffee mug:

- Be kind to yourself

- Nobody is perfect

- We all make mistakes

- Let's learn from our mistakes and help others do the same

I'd love to hear your examples and stories about putting those ideas to use, individually or in an organization.

Would you do me a favor?

Like all authors, I rely on online reviews to encourage future book purchases. Your opinion is invaluable. Would you take a few moments now to share your assessment of my book at the review site or book retailer of your choice? Your feedback will help other readers make informed decisions and support authors like me in the process. Thank you for your time and support—it means the world to me!

Please visit my website about the book, my podcast, and my general site:

mistakesbook.com
mistakespodcast.com
markgraban.com

Let's collaborate!

I am excited about the opportunity to work together and help your organization achieve its goals. I offer a range of in-person (or virtual) services, including speaking engagements, training sessions, and coaching programs that can help your leaders and teams thrive. My areas of practice and experience include psychological safety, mistake prevention, problem-solving, process improvement, and more. Additionally, I am trained and certified to administer and facilitate LeaderFactor's "4 Stages of Psychological Safety" methodology, which we can use to measure, learn, and improve together. Let's collaborate to create a culture of growth and success for your organization. Learn more about my services on my website, and let's get started today!

ENDNOTES

1. *My Favorite Mistake*, "Episode 1: Kevin Harrington & Mark Timm," markgraban.com/mistake1.

2. Berwick, Donald, MD, "Continuous Improvement as an Ideal in Health Care," *New England Journal of Medicine*, Jan. 1989.

3. Press Ganey, "Safety Solutions Starter®," oneumms.org/wp-content /uploads/Solutions-Starter-Safety.pdf.

4. Debevoise, Nell Derick, "Celebrating Errors Creates Psychological Safety in the Workplace," *Forbes.com*, forbes.com /sites/nelldebevoise/2021/05/29/celebrating-errors-creates -psychological-safety-in-the-workplace.

5. *My Favorite Mistake*, "Episode 154, Scott Hirsch," markgraban .com/mistake154.

6. *My Favorite Mistake*, "Episode 198, Kevin Goldsmith," markgraban .com/mistake198.

7. Goldsmith, Kevin, "Fail Safe, Fail Smart, Succeed! Part Four: My Biggest Failure," blog.kevingoldsmith.com/2020/12/30 /fail-safe-fail-smart-succeed-part-four-my-biggest-failure.

8. *My Favorite Mistake*, "Episode 196, Kevin Goldsmith," markgraban .com/mistake196.

9. *My Favorite Mistake*, "Special Episode: Dan Le Batard Show Personalities," markgraban.com/mistakeLAF.

10. *My Favorite Mistake*, "Episode 76, Matt Boos," markgraban.com /mistake76.

11. Edmondson, Amy C., *The Fearless Organization* (Hoboken, NJ: Wiley, 2018).

12. *Habitual Excellence*, "Episode 74, Brook Ward," valuecapturellc.com/he74.

13. Anderson, Katie. *Learning to Lead, Leading to Learn: Lessons from Toyota Leader Isao Yoshino on a Lifetime of Continuous Learning* (p. 21). Integrand Press. Kindle Edition.

14. Wilson Center, "Toyota in the U.S.: Learning from Our Past As We Prepare for the Future," wilsoncenter.org/event/toyota-the-us-learning-our-past-we-prepare-for-the-future.

15. Liker, Jeffrey K. *The Toyota Way, Second Edition: 14 Management Principles from the World's Greatest Manufacturer* (New York City: McGraw-Hill LLC).

16. *My Favorite Mistake*, "Episode 122, Joel Trammell," markgraban.com/mistake122.

17. *My Favorite Mistake*, "Episode 2, Will Hurd," markgraban.com/mistake2.

18. *My Favorite Mistake*, "Episode 200, Mark Graban," markgraban.com/mistake200.

19. *My Favorite Mistake*, "Episode 193, Kurt Wilkin," markgraban.com/mistake193.

20. *My Favorite Mistake*, "Episode 126, Amantha Imber," PhD, markgraban.com/mistake126.

21. *My Favorite Mistake*, "Episode 137, Daniel H. Pink," markgraban.com/mistake137.

22. Garrison Brothers, "Our Story," garrisonbros.com/our-story.

23. *My Favorite Mistake*, "Episode 11, Dan Garrison & Donnis Todd," markgraban.com/mistake11.

24. *My Favorite Mistake*, "Episode 153, Dr. Nicole Lipkin," markgraban.com/mistake153.

25. *My Favorite Mistake*, "Episode 172, Jim McCann," markgraban .com/mistake172.

26. *My Favorite Mistake*, "Episode 51, Lenny Walls," markgraban .com/mistake51.

27. Powell, Colin, *It Worked for Me* (New York City, Harper, 2012).

28. *My Favorite Mistake*, "Episode 117, Lynn Yap," markgraban.com /mistake117.

29. Ross, Karyn, *The Kind Leader: A Practical Guide to Eliminating Fear, Creating Trust, and Leading with Kindness* (New York City: Productivity Press, 2021).

30. *My Favorite Mistake*, "Episode 3, Karyn Ross," markgraban.com /mistake3.

31. *My Favorite Mistake*, "Episode 191, Dr. Julia DiGangi," markgraban .com/mistake191.

32. *My Favorite Mistake*, "Episode 128, Katie Anderson," markgraban .com/mistake128.

33. *My Favorite Mistake*, "Episode 183, Kristin Neff," markgraban .com/mistake183.

34. *My Favorite Mistake*, "Episode 103, Dr. Cheryl Lentz," markgraban .com/mistake103.

35. *My Favorite Mistake*, "Episode 169, Alisha Wielfaert," markgraban .com/mistake169.

36. *My Favorite Mistake*, "Episode 66, Mark Pett," markgraban.com /mistake66.

37. Deming, W. Edwards. *Out of the Crisis* (Cambridge, MA: The MIT Press, 1982).

38. *My Favorite Mistake*, "Episode 186, John Grout, PhD," markgraban .com/mistake186.

39. Patient Safety Network, "Alarm Fatigue," psnet.ahrq.gov /primer/alert-fatigue.

40. *My Favorite Mistake*, "Episode 31, Greg Jacobson, MD," markgraban.com/mistake31.

41. Detert, James R., Ethan R. Burris, and David A. Harrison, "Do Your Employees Think Speaking Up Is Pointless?" *Harvard Business Review*, hbr.org/2010/05/do-your-employees-think-speaki.

42. *My Favorite Mistake*, "Episode 70, David Mayer, PhD," markgraban .com/mistake70.

43. Mayer, David, MD, *How to Stay Safe When Entering the Healthcare System: A Physician Walks Across the Country to Raise Awareness of the Need to Improve Healthcare Safety* (Irvine, CA: Universal Publishers, 2022).

44. Classen, David, *et. al.*, "An Electronic Health Record-Based Real-Time Analytics Program for Patient Safety Surveillance and Improvement," *Health Affairs*, healthaffairs.org/doi/full/10.1377 /hlthaff.2018.0728.

45. Toussaint, John, MD, *On the Mend: Revolutionizing Healthcare to Save Lives and Transform the Industry* (Cambridge, MA, Lean Enterprise Institute: 2010).

46. Clark, Timothy R., PhD, *The 4 Stages of Psychological Safety* (Oakland, CA: Berrett-Koehler Publishers, 2020).

47. *My Favorite Mistake*, "Episode 5, Billy Taylor," markgraban.com /mistake5.

48. *My Favorite Mistake*, "Episode 67, Nika Kabiri," markgraban.com /mistake67.

49. *My Favorite Mistake*, "Episode 115, Kelly Cutchin," markgraban .com/mistake115.

50. *My Favorite Mistake*, Episode 83, Sabrina Malter," markgraban .com/mistake83.

51. *Lean Blog Interviews*, "Episode 356, Amy Edmondson, PhD," leanblog.org/356.

52. Edmondson, Amy, PhD, *The Fearless Organization: Creating Psychological Safety in the Workplace for Learning, Innovation, and Growth* (Hoboken, NJ: Wiley, 2018).

53. Liker, Jeff and Michael Hoseus, *Toyota Culture: The Heart and Soul of the Toyota Way* (New York City, McGraw-HIll: 2008).

54. *ibid.*

55. Schifferes, Steve, "The triumph of lean production," BBC News, bbc.co.uk/2/hi/business/6346315.stm.

56. *My Favorite Mistake*, "Episode 30, Isao Yoshino and Katie Anderson," markgraban.com/mistake30.

57. "NUMMI," *This American Life*, "Episode 403," thisamericanlife .org/403/nummi-2010.

58. Womack, James P., Jones, Daniel T., Roos, Daniel. *The Machine That Changed the World: The Story of Lean Production—Toyota's Secret Weapon in the Global Car Wars That Is Now Revolutionizing World Industry*, (New York City: Simon & Schuster, Inc., 1990).

59. Holusha, John, "G.M.'s Big Burden in Toyota Venture," *New York Times*, May 7, 1987, nytimes.com/1987/05/07/business/gm-s-big -burden-in-toyota-venture.html.

60. *My Favorite Mistake*, "Episode 147, Ken Segel," markgraban .com/mistake147.

61. Muller, David, "Facing $17 billion loss, color-coding helped Alan Mulally turn around Ford," mlive.com/auto/2016/07/alan_mulally _ralph_nader_induc.html.

62. *My Favorite Mistake*, "Episode 36, Stephen King," markgraban .com/mistake36.

63. Liker, Jeffrey K., Hoseus, Michael. *Toyota Culture: The Heart and Soul of the Toyota Way.* (New York City: McGraw-Hill LLC., 2008).

64. *My Favorite Mistake*, "Episode 186, John Grout, PhD," markgraban .com/mistake186.

65. *The Marshmallow Challenge*, marshmallowchallenge.com.

66. *My Favorite Mistake*, "Episode 22, Karen Martin," markgraban
.com/mistake22.

67. Obara, Samuel and Darril Wilburn, *Toyota by Toyota: Reflections
from the Inside Leaders on the Techniques That Revolutionized the
Industry* (New York City: Productivity Press, 2016).

68. *My Favorite Mistake*, "Episode 17, Melanie Parrish," markgraban
.com/mistake17.

69. *My Favorite Mistake*, "Episode 177, Emily Learing," markgraban
.com/mistake177.

70. *My Favorite Mistake*, "Episode 122, Joel Trammell," markgraban
.com/mistake122.

71. *My Favorite Mistake*, "Episode 78, Jeff Gothelf," markgraban
.com/mistake78.

72. *My Favorite Mistake*, "Episode 158, Karen Hold," markgraban
.com/mistake158.

73. *My Favorite Mistake*, "Episode 105, Andrea Jones," markgraban
.com/mistake105.

74. *My Favorite Mistake*, "Episode 181, Pamela Kellert," markgraban
.com/mistake181.

75. "John Toussaint MD on 'White Coat Leadership' vs.
Lean Leadership," youtube.com/watch?v=E-f0iDEVWM0
&ab_channel=MarkGraban.

76. Martini, Nico, *Texas Whiskey: A Rich History of Distilling Whiskey in
the Lone Star State*, (Kennebunkport, ME: Cider Mill Press, 2021).

77. *Habitual Excellence*, "Episode 74, Brook Ward," valuecapturellc
.com/HE74.

78. *My Favorite Mistake*, "Episode 96, Melissa Perri," markgraban
.com/mistake96.

79. Liker, Jeffrey K., Hoseus, Michael. *Toyota Culture: The Heart and
Soul of the Toyota Way*, (New York City: McGraw-Hill, 2008).

80. Oliva, Jacob, "Akio Toyoda Was a 'Terrible Person' at Age 20," Motor1.com, motor1.com/news/650350/akio-toyoda-terrible-person-twenty.

81. *My Favorite Mistake*, "Episode 94, David Meier," markgraban .com/mistake94.

82. *My Favorite Mistake*, "Episode 39, Matthew E. May," markgraban .com/mistake39.

83. Shook, John, *Managing to Learn: Using the A3 Management Process,* (Cambridge, MA: Lean Enterprise Institute, 2008).

84. Spear, Steven J., "Learning to Lead at Toyota," *Harvard Business Review*, hbr.org/2004/05/learning-to-lead-at-toyota.

85. "Matt Kresse & Vinuth Rai, Toyota: From Lean Manufacturing to Lean Startup," youtube.com/watch?v=78ajiBtkuQs.

86. Raymond Corporation, "Intralogistics Solutions Brochure," raymondcorp.com/optimization/lean-management.

87. *My Favorite Mistake*, "Episode 62, Keith Ingels," markgraban .com/mistake62.

88. Liker, Jeffrey, *The Toyota Way: 14 Management Principles from the World's Greatest Manufacturer,* (New York City: McGraw-Hill, 2004).

89. *My Favorite Mistake*, "Episode 31, Greg Jacbobson," markgraban .com/mistake31.